celebrate
advent
worship
& learning
resources

John Hendrix   Susan Meadors   David Miller

celebrate
advent
worship
& learning
resources

Illustrations by Robin Whitfield

SMYTH&HELWYS
PUBLISHING, INCORPORATED   MACON, GEORGIA

SMYTH&
HELWYS

Smyth & Helwys Publishing, Inc.
6316 Peake Road
Macon, Georgia 31210-3960
1-800-747-3016
©1999 by Smyth & Helwys Publishing

John Hendrix, Susan Meadors, David Miller

Library of Congress Cataloguing-in-Publication Data

Hendrix, John.
      Celebrate Advent: worship and learning resources/
      John Hendrix, Susan Meadors, David Miller.
      p.   cm.
      Includes bibliographical references.
      ISBN 1-57312-180-0 (alk. paper)
      1. Advent—Prayerbooks and devotions—English.
      2. Baptists—Liturgy—Texts.
      3. Worship programs.
      I. Meadors, Susan. II. Miller, David, 1952 Mar. 1. III. Title.
      BV40.H45 1999
      264'.061—dc21   98-30884
                                                        CIP

ISBN 978-1-57312-180-4

"People, Look East" reprinted by permission. Music from *Oxford Book of Carols* (Oxford University Press, 1928). Text by Eleanor Farjeon, *The Children's Bells* (London: David Higham Assoc./27.10.98).

Contents

Educational Activities

Preface

People, look east and sing today:
Love is on the way.

The gifts of Christmas come in unexpected ways. Our gift for the Advent season at Northside Baptist Church, Clinton, Mississippi, came from these words in our hymnal. During the Advent season we turned our eyes toward the east and sang a new song, "People, Look East." This hymn calls on different parts of creation to prepare for the coming Christ child.

The first three notes, sung in unison, punctuate the call to action and readiness. The gentle swing of the rhythm and the cheerful and majestic D-major harmonies fit the theme of creation making ready—being busy, looking, singing, announcing—for "Love the Lord is on the way."

Speaking and singing of Christ in these ways gave us new ways of seeing ourselves. "Beloved, we are God's children now; what we will be has not yet been revealed. What we do know is this: when he is revealed, we will be like him, for we see Christ as he is" (1 John 3:2).

This book is a collection of resources to help churches celebrate Advent. It is built around a central theme based on an English carol that provides the images for each of the four weeks of Advent. This Advent celebration was developed for our church's use during December 1996. For publication, it has been revised and supplemented with explanatory and educational materials.

These materials are the product of many hands. While the pastoral staff of the church developed the basic ideas for the services, implementation of them required the assistance of the worship committee and many other talented people in the congregation. It would be a mistake, therefore, for any church to attempt to duplicate exactly the material within this book. Instead, this book should serve as a guide to inspire creative thinking that heightens the worship experience. Liturgy means "common work." The goal for this book, then, is to further the common work of worship in other churches.

People, Look East

BESANÇON 8.7.9.8.8.7

Eleanor Farjeon (1881–1965)
As in *Oxford Book of Carols*, 1964

French folk melody
Harm. Martin Shaw (1875–1958)

1. Peo - ple, look east. The time is near Of the crown-ing of the year. Make your house fair as you are a - ble, Trim the hearth and set the ta - ble. Peo-ple, look east and sing to - day: Peo-ple, look east: Love the guest is on the way.

2. Fur - rows, be glad. Though earth is bare, One more seed is plant - ed there: Give up your strength the seed to nour - ish, That in course the flower may flour - ish. Love the rose is on the way.

3. Birds, though you long have ceased to build, Guard the nest that must be filled. E - ven the hour when wings are fro - zen God for fledg - ing time has cho - sen. Love the bird is on the way.

4. Stars, keep the watch. When night is dim One more light the bowl shall brim, Shin - ing be - yond the frost - y weath - er, Bright as sun and moon to - geth - er. Peo-ple, look east: Love the star is on the way.

5. Angels, announce with shouts of mirth
   Christ who brings new life to earth.
   Set every peak and valley humming
   With the word, the Lord is coming.
   People, look east and sing today:
   Love the Lord is on the way.

Acknowledgments

One of the joys of working with church staffs and committees is watching the diverse ways in which members contribute to events and projects. We express our love for one another by learning to look together in the same direction. When we focused our eyes toward "looking east," the gifts of the people at Northside emerged, and we began our own journey toward the stable in Bethlehem, bringing and offering our gifts.

We have happily identified ourselves as a Baptist church that follows the liturgical Christian calendar. The Advent season awakens our congregation as perhaps no other season does. If we mentioned all the musicians, choirs, committees, and lay worship leaders, we would be naming the whole congregation. However, there is a stable working core of people who provide leadership for all our seasonal events.

The worship committee provides directional planning. Tom Hunt, John Meadors, David Miller, Anna Rosenthal, Cynthia Tucker, and Duewayne Tullos made up the worship committee that spearheaded the emphasis on "People, Look East." Lida Stark is the Minister of Music and overall music coordinator. Kathy Dent and Jo Ann Pope are the instrumentalists. Jo Ann provided the background and comments on the hymn "People, Look East." Robin Whitfield, a promising young artist, captured the power of the hymn's images in her creative drawings. Jan Hurt's banner illuminated Robin's artwork on cloth and canvas. The epigraphs at the beginning of each worship service were written by John Meadors, Linda McComb, Jerrell Hutson, and Duewayne Tullos. We also express appreciation to Cindy Budzinski, church secretary, and Lucy Rushing for manuscript preparation and development.

As with all church projects, we had our peaks and valleys. Thus, we know some of the meanings in the last stanza of the hymn.

> *Set every peak and valley humming*
> *With the word, the Lord is coming.*
> *People, look east and sing today:*
> *Love the Lord is on the way.*

Preparing for Advent

Preparation for Advent at our church often begins nearly a year in advance. As soon as one Christmas celebration ends, the worship staff begins thinking about the next year's theme and activities. Like many churches, the weeks preceding Christmas are busy ones for the members of our congregation. School activities, shopping, church parties, choir concerts, housecleaning, and baking crowd the calendar. Our celebration of Advent, however, has become a meaningful way of disciplining ourselves to prepare for the celebration of Christmas as a Christian holiday.

Each year it seems as if the activities associated with Christmas begin earlier and earlier. Tree decorations are for sale before November. Carols can be heard over the loudspeakers of grocery stores long before Thanksgiving. Many Christians have sought for ways to separate themselves from the materialism and consumerism represented by this rush to Christmas. At our church, Advent, with its slow and steady rhythms, has become a way to take the time to prepare. Our congregation has learned to look forward to some traditional activities such as lighting the Advent candles and singing the Advent hymns.

Many churches that traditionally have paid little attention to the liturgical calendar are rediscovering the seasons of the church year. Among those beginning to reexamine this ancient tradition, Advent seems to be a natural place to begin. As the beginning of the church year, it corresponds to a period when many churches already have special services and emphases. Advent, however, is not just another way to celebrate Christmas. It is a holy season all its own with its own history and focus.

Understanding the Season

Although Advent is the ecclesiastical season many Christians are now discovering, it was one of the last to be added to the church year. The celebration of Easter, weekly on Sunday and annually during Passover, was the first set observance that marked Christian time as distinct from other time. To that celebration was added the Holy Week services, and then Lent, the season of preparation for Holy Week. The rest of the year was known as ordinary time, punctuated only by the Christmas celebration in some areas of Christendom.

By the fourth century, many churches were celebrating a period of preparation for Christmas similar in form and length to the Lenten fasts. This season, called Advent, was a period of four to six weeks marking the preparation for the celebration of Christ's appearance, the Christ Mass, or Christmas. During the fourth century, the four-week period of preparation was adopted throughout the Western Church. It is a period of fasting and prayer, much like Lent. Through the following centuries, however, Advent lost many of its strict disciplines and became a period of celebratory anticipation.

Advent has retained some of its original sense of fasting and prayer, evident in hymns, some written in a minor key, and in prayers of confession or repentance in anticipation of the coming of the Lord. "O Come, O Come, Emmanuel" and "Come, Thou Long-Expected Jesus" are two traditional Advent hymns. They are quite different from the joyous nature of most Christmas carols.

With each season of the year the church told part of the story of Jesus Christ. Since Advent was the season to prepare for Christ's birth, certain narrative elements became associated with the services of Advent. The prophecies of the Old Testament formed the first part of the narrative. The church rehearsed the words of Genesis, Isaiah, Malachi, and others that told of a coming messiah. The annunciation to Mary and her submissive response to the Almighty were other elements important to the Advent season. Joseph's submission to God's dream and the Bethlehem journey leading up to the birth were also part of the celebration, as were the angels who played an integral role in the birth narrative itself.

Many contemporary Advent services are built around four abstract elements: hope, peace, joy, and love. These have scriptural antecedents, of course, and echo many of the sentiments expressed during the Christmas celebration. Some churches choose to focus on these themes because they are then freed from the slow narrative pace of the Advent stories. In this volume we have included both abstract and narrative elements.

This season then, historically and practically, is one of preparation, prayer, and story. It is a different way to approach Christmas. It pauses to consider the divine and human elements that come together to make the birth of Christ miraculous. It reflects on characters who saw visions, submitted themselves to the divine plan, and worshiped through their very lives. Advent can be a season when we find ourselves stopping and reflecting often on our way to Bethlehem.

Introducing the Season

Any change in worship style or direction must be made slowly and carefully. Churches that know little about the church year may find a celebration of Advent strange and disruptive to their normal Christmas traditions. Others, however, will discover what many of us have discovered, that Advent is a wonderful alternative to the way those outside the church celebrate this holy holiday.

Advent celebrations at Northside Baptist Church have evolved slowly over several years to the form shared in this book. We suggest that worship leaders and church staff move slowly through the first couple of years. Education and explanation are key ingredients to a meaningful Advent celebration. To assist worship planners, we have included educational materials that can be implemented in a Sunday morning or evening or Wednesday evening setting. Some of this material is related directly to the theme of the worship services, whereas some involves the Advent season itself.

You might begin to celebrate Advent by introducing one or two of the traditional symbols connected with the season. A banner can provide a visual focal point for the four Sundays preceding Christmas. Hung in front of the sanctuary, the picture on the banner becomes part of the reflection of Advent. Another means of introducing the season is the lighting of candles in the Advent wreath.

The Advent wreath is a variation on the traditional evergreen wreath signifying the everlasting life and circle of eternity that has no beginning and no end. Five candles traditionally are added to the wreath. Three purple candles and one pink candle are on the perimeter, while one white candle is in the center. The colors are significant. Ideally, the four outer candles move from a dark purple to light pink to symbolize the approach of Christmas. Most Advent candle kits today, however, include only three similarly colored candles and one pink candle. One candle on the outer wreath is lit on the first Sunday. Two candles are lit on the second; three, on the third; and on the fourth, the pink candle is lit along with the three purple candles. On Christmas Eve the white candle, or little Christ candle, is lit, symbolizing the arrival of Christmas.

The Advent wreath might be the focus of children's sermons during the Advent season, or the candles might be lit as a special part of the service. However they are used, the banner and wreath can easily be used to educate people as they mark the movement of time for a congregation through the four-week period. A variation on the traditional Christmas tree can also help educate a congregation about Christian time and Christian symbols.

A chrismon tree is decorated with "Christ monograms," images historically and traditionally related to Christ. These include the ichthus, the lamb, the lamp, various forms of crosses, the anchor, and many others. Activities related to making and explaining these symbols can be developed for all age groups in the congregation.

Everyone in the congregation should be invited to participate in the planning and presentation of the Advent celebration. Banner makers, flower arrangers, lay readers, decorators, devotional writers, artists, and others work together at our church. After the theme is chosen, usually by the pastor and worship staff, the ideas are related to those gifted in various areas for implementation. Delegating responsibilities requires a certain amount of trust and freedom, but it ultimately enhances the worship experience for everyone. Advent becomes a community worship experience and truly fulfills the meaning of the word, "liturgy," a common work.

Adapting the Services

The services and materials in this book were created specifically for use at Northside Baptist Church. In many ways, however, all worship is both universal and distinctly local. In celebrating Advent, there are universal themes of hope, anticipation, preparation, and fulfillment. How individual churches express these themes will depend upon the creativity and gifts of each congregation.

These resources, then, should be seen as suggestions. The words, devotionals, prayers, music, and educational activities should give others inspiration and ideas of their own for celebrating Advent. These resources can be readily adapted for a family celebration of Advent or for a para-church group that meets regularly throughout the season. With some advance planning, an Advent booklet can be assembled that includes art work and devotionals and orders of the worship services for each Sunday. It was from such a booklet that *Celebrate Advent* came.

The worship services in this book are based on the hymn "People, Look East." Worship planning began with the words of the hymn. Its five stanzas provided a natural focus for each of the five services. Each of the first four stanzas uses a different metaphor for Christ: guest, rose, bird, and star. The fifth stanza refers directly to the Lord's coming. The congregation learned this hymn, adding a stanza each Sunday, until the entire hymn could be sung on Christmas Eve.

On the first Sunday of Advent we set the communion table with the best china and silver as if planning for a special meal with friends. The art work reflected the image of an open door that might welcome the stranger. At each point in the service we were reminded that Advent requires a welcoming spirit.

On the second Sunday the ancient carol "Lo, How a Rose E'er Blooming" provided a wonderful musical counterpoint to the words of our Advent hymn. In the foyer of the church an array of roses provided a spot of beauty in the cold December air.

The focus of the third Sunday was originally one of the most difficult images to develop, but it became especially meaningful as we explored images of flight and nesting—making our homes ready for the birth of Christ.

On the fourth Sunday nearest to Christmas, the shining star seemed a natural symbol as we anticipated the rising of the Daystar in our hearts. The service on that Sunday set the stage for the 11 PM Christmas Eve observance. We heard the ancient texts read, sang the old carols, and as Christmas Day approached, received the elements of communion.

Much work is involved in our Advent celebration, but the rewards are immense. Worship is an offering we make to God collectively. Introducing Advent to a local congregation and implementing its elements is but one avenue through which worship can occur. As a staff, we have found the elements of Advent to be especially helpful in aiding our worship. And it is in that sense we offer these resources to others.

Orders of Worship

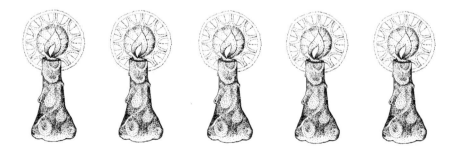

Love
the Guest Is on the Way

This time of year we talk about the coming of Jesus. We go so far as to call this the "Advent season." Based on the decorations (and our grocery bills!), it appears we really are expecting him to come into our homes. The warm colors and savory aromas we create are designed to be inviting to our guests. But they are more than inviting; they are enticing.

Guests come into our homes during this season more often than at any other time of the year. And, of course, Jesus comes, too. For most of our guests, the enticement is no trap; they go home well fed and well pleased with our hospitality. But Jesus stays long after he has worn out his welcome. Eventually we treat him shabbily. In the end we crucify him.

In the Talmud, Rabbi Jacob says, "A person, on whose account God has to inflict punishment on another, will not be admitted into the presence of God" (*Shabbat* 149b). To explain this difficult teaching, Rabbi Louis Finkelstein says, "The underlying principle . . . is the doctrine that a victim of injustice falls short of the idea of Judaism to the extent that he fails to obtain divine forgiveness for the person who acted unjustly toward him" Behold the King of the Jews!

—John Meadors

The Worship of God

The First Sunday of Advent

Greetings and Announcements

Opening Sentences

Pastor:	People, look east!
People:	**Love the guest is on the way.**
Pastor:	Prepare!
People:	**Prepare!**
Pastor:	Prepare the way of the Lord.
Women:	Brothers, sweep the floors and set the tables.
Men:	Sisters, tend the fires and light the candles.
All:	**Let us make our houses as fair as we are able.**
Pastor:	Love the guest is on the way.
People:	**Let us prepare the way of the Lord.**

Choral Introit   Allen

Prepare Ye the Way of the Lord

Prelude   Handel

Overture to *Messiah*

*Processional Hymn   Weissel

Lift Up Your Heads, Ye Mighty Gates

Advent Collect (unison)

O God, who in your coming found only a stable welcome, help us, we pray, to be holy hosts for you. Help us, your body, your church, to show forth your presence in this lonely world. Emmanuel, God with us, the table spread before us has everything we need; we long to sit and be with you. Prepare us, even as we are preparing for you, O Heavenly Guest. Amen.

13

Reading from the Old Testament

Isaiah 40:3-11

Leader: This is the Word of the Lord.
People: Thanks be to God.

Morning Carol

Shaw

People, Look East

Reading from the New Testament

Ephesians 2:11-22

Leader: This is the Word of the Lord.
People: Thanks be to God.

A Reading

George Herbert

Love III

Love bade me welcome: yet my soul drew back,
Guilty of dust and sin.
But quick-eyed Love, observing me grow slack
From my first entrance in,
Drew nearer to me, sweetly questioning
If I lacked anything.

"A guest," I answered, "worthy to be here."
Love said, "You shall be he."
"I, the unkind, ungrateful? Ah, my dear,
I cannot look on thee."
Love took my hand and smiling did reply,
"Who made the eyes but I?"

"Truth, Lord; but I have marred them: let my shame
Go where it doth deserve."
"And know you not," says Love, "who bore the blame?"
"My dear, then I will serve."
"You must sit down," says Love, "and taste my meat."
So I did sit and eat.

Musical Interlude

Handel

Pastoral Symphony from *Messiah*

Morning Prayer

O God, we wonder where you might show up this Christmas season. We are beginning our preparation, looking east, knowing a guest is on the way. Somehow we will discover that you are among us, but we wonder where and when that will be. So we're going to fix up our homes and church. But when guests are coming, they usually come by invitation, and we don't like surprises. We will hold people at our doors if they seem a little strange. Forgive us if we seem so comfortable in our preparation that we close our doors to surprise. But you have never entered our world without surprising us. Our Old Testament ancestors thought you would come as a warrior doing battle with all their enemies, never dreaming you would come as a helpless infant.

So today we prepare for your coming, knowing that there will be many distractions, and we want to get it just right. Our church is busy today with activity, but we will hardly be ready for surprise. So, if you're going to come some time other than 10:30 on Sunday morning, help us to be ready to hear and see you. And if you do not show up in our homes but in some abandoned covering for the homeless, I seriously doubt we will be there. Most likely, your coming will seem a little strange, so prepare our hearts to welcome the stranger. Amen.

Offertory   Vivaldi
Largo from "Winter Season"

Doxology
   O Heavenly Guest, we lift our praise,
   We wait for you, Ancient of Days.
   We've set the table, made the meal.
   Praise God! For here is Love revealed. Amen.

Children's Time
   The Lighting of the Advent Candle
   (4 and 5 year-olds may then exit to children's worship)

*Reading from the Gospel   Matthew 25:31-46
   Leader: This is the Gospel of the Lord.
   People: Thanks be to God.

15

Ministry of Music   Pachebel
Canon in D

Sermon
"Love the Guest Is on the Way"

Sanctus

The Mystery of Communion
The Bread of Life
The Cup of Salvation

*Hymn of Response   Wesley
Come, Thou Long-Expected Jesus

Affirmation of Christian Decision (unison)
We affirm you in your Christian decision and celebrate your place in the family of God. We accept our responsibility to help you grow into the fullness of Christ. We offer ourselves to be your family, to surround you with God's kind of love.

Closing Sentences

Pastor:	Out of the silence, out of the weariness, out of chaos, and even out of cynicism, comes a voice. The Lord is coming; God is near.
People:	**Love the Guest is on the way!**
Pastor:	Thanks be to God for the indescribable gift.
People:	**Thanks be to God. Amen.**

*Closing Hymn   Shaw
People, Look East

Postlude   Vivaldi
Third Movement from "Winter Season"

*Congregation Standing

Love
the Rose Is on the Way

From the hymn "People, Look East," I learned about the Advent rose, a small rose that grows in Palestine. Its circlets are deep yellow; the petal tips are white; the rays at the center of the petals are red; and the insets between the petals are green.

Whenever I see a rose, it demands my attention. Its beauty and message will not go unnoticed. I see the roses a volunteer places in the intensive care waiting room at the hospital. I see the roses a family member grew and arranged to celebrate a wedding. I see the single rose that welcomes a new baby into the church family. I see the roses a family grew and often shared with me.

The advent of Christ into the world and into our lives as individuals is like noticing a beautiful wild rose. It demands our attention and reminds us of God's abiding presence, sometimes growing in darkness, sometimes blooming in grace and beauty for all to see. We recognize our blessedness and choose to notice the rose. During the Advent season, notice the rose.

—Linda Snell McComb

"The Wild Rose" by Wendell Berry

Sometimes hidden from me
In daily custom and in trust,
So that I live by you unaware
As by the beating of my heart.

Suddenly you flare in my sight,
A wild rose blooming at the edge
Of thicket, grace and light
Where yesterday was only shade.

And once more I am blessed,
Choosing again what I chose before.
And once more I am blessed,
Choosing again what I chose before.

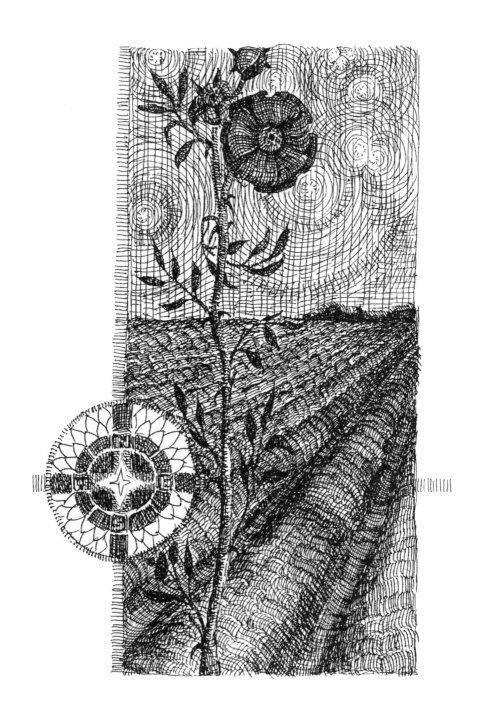

18

The Worship of God

The Second Sunday of Advent

Greetings and Announcements

Opening Sentences

Leader:	People, look east!
People:	**Love like a rose is on the way**.
Leader:	In the cold and dark December, behold, the Rose of Sharon buds.
Women:	A miracle in the winter,
Men:	A tender flower blooms.
Leader:	Everywhere God comes, the wilderness blossoms.
People:	**In hard and frozen hearts love grows**.
Leader:	Love like a rose is on the way.
People:	**May God blossom forth in us**.

Prelude   Held

Of the Father's Love Begotten

*Processional Hymn   Wesley

Come, Thou Long-Expected Jesus

Advent Collect (unison)

O God, who in your coming found a wilderness, dry and barren, help us, we pray, to prepare our hardhearted ground for you. Flood our hearts with forgiveness, and shine on them in mercy. Plant your seed within us until our barrenness is no more. Emmanuel, God with us, your abundance is everything we need. Send your fragrance over us, O Rose of Sharon. Amen.

Reading from the Old Testament   Isaiah 35:1-10

Leader:	This is the Word of the Lord.
People:	**Thanks be to God**.

Morning Carol   Shaw

People, Look East

Reading from the New Testament   2 Corinthians 2:14-17
    Leader: This is the Word of the Lord.
    People: **Thanks be to God.**

A Reading   Christina G. Rosetti

In the Bleak Midwinter

In the bleak midwinter,
Frosty wind made moan,
Earth stood hard as iron,
Water like a stone;
Snow had fallen, snow on snow,
Snow on snow,
In the bleak midwinter,
Long ago.

Our God, heaven cannot hold Him,
Nor earth sustain;
Heaven and earth shall flee away,
When He comes to reign:
In the bleak midwinter,
A stable place sufficed,
The Lord God incarnate,
Jesus Christ.

Angels and archangels,
May have gathered there,
Cherubim and seraphim,
Thronged the air;
But His mother only,
In her maiden bliss,
Worshiped the beloved,
With a kiss.

What can I give Him,
Poor as I am?
If I were a shepherd,
I would bring a lamb;
If I were a wise man,
I would do my part;
Yet what I can I give Him:
Give my heart.

Musical Interlude   Ham
In the Bleak Midwinter

Morning Prayer
Almighty God, we look, and we pray that love is on the way. The year
rushes to its close, and we are weary of it. Everywhere are the signs of
ending, and a cold winter is upon us. The earth is barren, the fields are
bare, the trees are gray and leafless; it is resting time and waiting time. It
is also time to look for your coming.

We strain our ears and hearts for angel sounds, for an infant cry and
gentle lowing of cattle, for soft heavenly lullabies. In the bleakness of
midwinter we hunger for sounds that call us to warmth, hints that even
the desert within us will blossom forth into springtime. Can our small
seeds of faith bring forth the bloom of your love here in this place?

Is it planting time? Teach us to busy ourselves with sewing seeds of
kindness and grace, of forgiveness and understanding.

Is it time to nourish the seed? Lead us to be fed by the Spirit and to
drink deeply from the cup of fellowship and the water of life.

Is it time to harvest, separating wheat from weeds, the rose from the
thorns? Help us to simplify our lives, to rid ourselves of the glitter, gloss,
and tinsel of merrymaking and enter the quiet stable for peace and rest
and adoration.

O come, let us adore you, O God in Christ, rose among the thorns.
As our hearts swell to greet you, be born in us again we pray. Amen.

Offertory   Pethel
It Came upon a Midnight Clear

21

Doxology

O Rose of Winter, bloom, we pray,
Within our hearts and show the way,
That we can grow and bud and flower,
We praise thee, God, this very hour. Amen.

Children's Time

The Lighting of the Advent Candle
(4 and 5 year-olds may then exit to children's worship)

*Reading from the Gospel   Matthew 13:24-30

Leader: This is the Gospel of the Lord
People: Thanks be to God.

Ministry of Music   Allen

Lo, How a Rose E'er Blooming

Sermon

"Love the Rose Is on the Way"

*Hymn of Response   Benson

O Sing a Song of Bethlehem

Affirmation of Christian Decision (unison)

We affirm you in your Christian decision and celebrate your place in the
family of God. We accept our responsibility to help you grow into the
fullness of Christ. We offer ourselves to be your family, to surround you
with God's kind of love.

Closing Sentences

Pastor: Our ground is cold and barren.
**People: Our hearts are often hard. More like weeds than
flowers, with shallow roots, we hold on, fearing the
Gardener's hand.**

A Period of Silence

Pastor: But out of the cold hard clay of humanity comes God's
            Rose; Love is blossoming all around us.
People: **The desert becomes a garden, the wilderness a place**
            of joy. Love like a rose is on the way.
Pastor: Thanks be to God for the fragrance of forgiveness.
People: **Thanks be to God. Amen.**

*Closing Hymn   Shaw

People, Look East

Postlude   Buouo

A Christmas Medley

*Congregation Standing

Love
the Bird Is on the Way

Humans have long been fascinated with birds and have used them to express concepts and emotions, for example, "birds of a feather," the wise old owl," and "a bird in the hand."

We use the eagle to represent political and military might. We consider the dove to be the symbol of peace and love. And just as the dove came to be used in the temple sacrifices because of its gentleness and purity, Jesus was born to become our sacrifice and the personification of peace and love.

"And a dove was sent out . . ."

—Jerrell Hutson

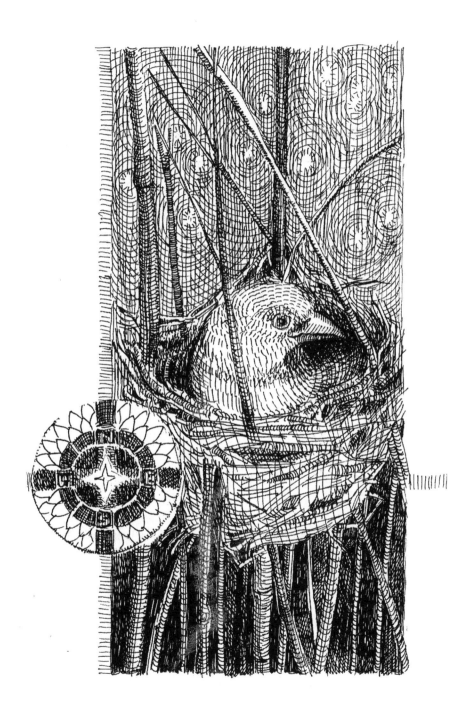

The Worship of God
The Third Sunday of Advent

Greetings and Announcements

Opening Sentences

Leader:	People, look east!
People:	**Love like a bird is on the way.**
Leader:	Behold, the Son of Righteousness is rising with healing in his wings.
People:	**Behold, God gathers us all under those wings, the way a hen gathers her young.**
Men:	Like a dove, calling to its mate,
Women:	Like an eagle, flying on the wind,
All:	**Love like a bird is on the way.**
Leader:	Listen for the beating of wings.

Prelude Wyrtzen

Sonata of Christmas

*Processional Hymn Helmore

O Come, O Come, Emmanuel

Advent Collect (unison)

O God, who in your coming found no place to lay your head, nest yourself in us, we pray. Be born in us and teach us, like little birds, to tweedle praise, to cry to you, to learn to fly on wings of faith. Emmanuel, God with us, your love of us is all we need. Spread your bright wings over us, we pray. Amen.

Reading from the Old Testament Deuteronomy 32:7-12

Leader:	This is the Word of the Lord.
People:	**Thanks be to God.**

Morning Carol Shaw

People, Look East

Reading from the Old Testament   Malachi 3:16; 4:2

Leader: This is the Word of the Lord.
People: Thanks be to God.

A Reading   Gerard Manly Hopkins

The Windhover: To Christ Our Lord

I caught this morning morning's minion,
kingdom of daylight's dauphin,
dapple-dawn-drawn Falcon, in his riding
Of the rolling level underneath him steady air, and striding
High there, how he rung upon the rein of a wimpling wing
In his ecstasy! then off, off forth on swing,
As a skate's heel sweeps smooth on a bow-bend: the hurl and gliding
Rebuffed the big wind. My heart in hiding
Stirred for a bird—the achieve of, the mastery of the thing!

Brute beauty and valour and act, oh, air, pride, plume, here
Buckle! and the fire that breaks from thee then, a billion
Times told lovelier, more dangerous, O my chevalier!

No wonder of it: sheer plod makes plough down sillion
Shine, and blue-bleak embers, ah my dear,
Fall, gall themselves, and gash gold-vermillion.

Advent Carol   Kaan

Down to Earth, As a Dove

Morning Prayer

O God, we confess: sometimes we think we can fly! Of course, we know
it's only in our dreams, but there we go, freed from the confining aspects
of limited space and ready for any journey that would call us. We have
our days when we long for that kind of freedom and the exhilaration of
being cut loose.

But perhaps there is a deeper longing in us. There is a longing for
sanctuary, a safe, warm, protected place, a place of refuge where we are
cared for, nurtured, and loved. We understand the Psalmist's longing for
your dwelling places. "Even the sparrow finds a home, and a swallow a

nest for herself, where she may lay her young." Jesus saw himself as a mother bird constantly calling us to himself, knowing full well that being close to him would bring us close to one another.

So gathering is our first act of worship. In gathering, we give evidence that Jesus is alive in our hearts and in our midst. Even when two or three gather, there he is among us. In gathering, in assembling, in meeting, we model the Christian life. In gathering, we make questionable all artificial distinctions of age, race, sex, or status. We find a different way of living and not one we expected. Why is that so?

We also confess that longing to be free of all constraints, to go it alone and find our own way. We don't realize how dangerous it is out there when we are scattered. We can still hear the call of the mother bird to gather, but we do not respond. We forget who we are and where we belong. Jesus said, "How I longed to gather you as a mother bird gathers her brood under her wings, but you are not willing."

And yet you still choose to come into our midst, knowing full well that it will take laying down your life to protect us, choosing to be nothing more and nothing less than a mother bird. If all the destructive forces get to us, they will have to get to you first. And that's exactly what happens. It's the price you pay for finally gathering all of creation together in him. We offer our prayer in his name. Amen.

Offertory Honeycutt

Infant Holy, Infant Lowly

Doxology
Praise God, you people, rise and sing.
See, Love is coming on the wing,
Nest yourself in us, Lord, we pray,
Be born anew this very day. Amen.

Children's Time
The Lighting of the Advent Candle
(4 and 5 year-olds may then exit to children's worship)

*Reading from the Gospel   Luke 13:31-34
    Leader: This is the Gospel of the Lord.
    People: Thanks be to God.

Sermon
            "Love the Bird Is on the Way"

*Hymn of Response   French Carol
            Let All Mortal Flesh Keep Silence

Affirmation of Christian Decision (unison)
We affirm you in your Christian decision and celebrate your place in the
family of God. We accept our responsibility to help you grow into the
fullness of Christ. We offer ourselves to be your family, to surround you
with God's kind of love.

Closing Sentences
    Leader: Like an eagle tends her nest,
    People: Like a hen gathers her young,
    Leader: So Love Incarnate comes into a world, full and
               rebellious.

A Period of Silence
    Leader: This is our fledgling time.
    People: In the middle of winter we are born anew.
    All: Help us to rise up, on wings, like eagles ourselves.
               Help us in fragile faith to fly to you.
    Leader: Thanks be to God for the freedom of the flight of faith.
    People: Thanks be to God. Amen.

*Closing Hymn   Shaw
            People, Look East

Postlude   Kelsey
            Hark, the Herald Angels Sing

*Congregation Standing

Love
the Star Is on the Way

*There is not enough darkness in all the world
to put out the light of one small candle.*

These words, found in the epilogue of Arthur Gordon's book *A Touch of Wonder*, are not so moving for their poetry and imagery, but they contain a wonderful truth. In moments of dark discouragement we can always cling to the candle of certain memories, particularly associations with those by whom we are deeply loved—our friends, family, and children.

Such is the light of the star that shone so bright long ago over the Palestinian countryside and led the magi to the Christ child. The consciousness of this star can still lead to God's ultimate expression of love.

—Duewayne Tullos

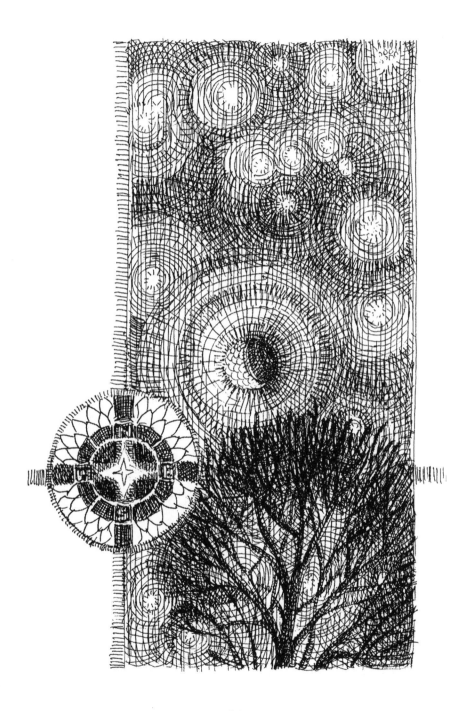

The Worship of God
The Fourth Sunday of Advent

Greetings and Announcements

Opening Sentences

Leader:	People, look east!
People:	**Love like a star is on the way.**
Leader:	A star shall rise out of Jacob.
People:	**A light to all people, a hope to the nations.**
Women:	Star light,
Men:	Star bright,
All:	**Brightest star that was seen that night. Come and rise within our hearts, rise and never set, O Bright and Morning Star. Amen.**

Prelude Manz
Still, Still, Still

*Processional Hymn Neale
Creator of the Stars of Night

Advent Collect (unison)

O God, who in your coming found a world cold and dark with sin, shine forth in our hearts. Light of the World, enlighten us that we, too, might burn with holy fire, not alone but in constellations. Emmanuel, God with us, your bright presence is all we need. Shine your holy starlight over us, we pray. Amen.

Reading from the Old Testament Isaiah 9:2, 6-7

Leader:	This is the Word of the Lord.
People:	**Thanks be to God.**

Morning Carol Shaw
People, Look East

Reading from the New Testament   Revelation 1:9-20; 22-16
    Leader: This is the Word of the Lord.
    People: **Thanks be to God.**

A Reading   Joan Johnson

A Prayer for Each Day's Journey

Touch me, Lord,
With the promise of your dawning.
Prince of the Morning,
Rising swift and sure.
Breaking through the shadows
Of my fitful sleeping,
Bring me to awakening
Of your great love once more.

Touch me, Lord,
With the power of your rejoicing.
Day star of the noontime,
Rising on the wave
Of your hope and glory
In your true light our story,
Unfolding realm of brightness
Your Spirit comes to save.

. . . .

Be there, Lord,
When the nightfall veils my vision.
Light in my darkness,
Guide me on the way.
Bear me on the ocean
In the depths of your compassion.
Bring me safe to harbour
At the closing of my day.

Musical Interlude   Campbell

O Come, O Come, Emmanuel

33

Morning Prayer

O God, the magi caught sight of Christ's star, looking east. But there were thousands of others who did not see the star. Maybe they were not looking for it. Maybe they were so trapped in their jobs trying to make ends meet or so busy with their parties and engagements that it never occurred to them to look up. We never see the stars when we are so grounded, plodding along with our heads bowed, our bodies bent and shoulders drooping.

Yet almost all of us were dreamers once. But life wears us down and erodes our dreams unless some star startles us beyond our hurts and disappointments. But there it was, a light breaking in the east, shining away in the night, and only a few saw it. Perhaps Jesus' unpredictable friend named Peter understood our dilemma. Peter referred to Jesus as "a lamp shining in a dark place, until the day dawns and the morning star rises in your hearts." Perhaps he understood that the star needs to rise in our hearts before we can see it shining in the sky.

So this morning we pray that the light of Christ will push the shadows away that continue to linger causing doubt and fear. We pray that this light will comfort us through nights of loneliness when sleep does not grant us escape from the cares and burdens that plague us. May that star remind our hearts that nothing in all creation can ultimately separate us from the love of God in Christ Jesus.

O God, light our dark skies. Provide a lantern for our footsteps. Shine a beacon to guide our steps. Enlighten our paths and keep us from falling. Shine on us; shine on us. Let the light of Jesus shine on us. We pray this in the name of the one who was light and in him was no darkness at all. Amen.

Offertory   Pethel
The First Noel

Doxology
O Bright and Morning Star, now shine
With light from you, you we will find;
Set us afire with holy light;
Help us to burn through this dark night. Amen.

Children's Time
The Lighting of the Advent Candle
(4 and 5 year-olds may then exit to children's worship)

*Reading from the Gospel   John 1:1-5, 9-14
Leader: This is the Gospel of the Lord.
People: Thanks be to God.

Sermon

"Love the Star Is on the Way"

*Hymn of Response   Luther
Savior of the Nations, Come

Affirmation of Christian Decision (unison)
We affirm you in your Christian decision and celebrate your place in the family of God. We accept our responsibility to help you grow into the fullness of Christ. We offer ourselves to be your family, to surround you with God's kind of love.

Closing Sentences
Leader: The people who sat in darkness . . .
People: That would be us, blinded by sin and death, until the whole world seems shrouded in shadows.

A Period of Silence
Leader: The people who sat in darkness have seen a great light.
People: Sometimes gradual, like dawn,
Sometimes startling, like lightning,
Sometimes beautiful, like fire,
Sometimes constant, like a star—
God comes to us.
Leader: And God is coming to us, light and love incarnate. Thanks be to God for light and love, for the star out of Jacob.
People: Thanks be to God. Amen.

*Closing Hymn   Shaw
People, Look East

Postlude   Sharp
Once In Royal David's City

*Congregation Standing

Love
the Lord Is on the Way

It is finally here. After months of preparation and expectation, Christmas Eve is upon us. As all who await the birth of a new baby, we feel today the same extreme emotions of excitement and fear, anticipation and dread. The work is done; the house is prepared; the gifts are wrapped. And as we lay out our stockings, we lay down our lives to receive the gifts of joy, peace, and grace from the Christ child. We are ready. In unison, but different voices, we shout:

> "Welcome, long-awaited Little One!"
> "*Seja bemvindo!*"
> "*Sois bienvenu!*"
>
> —Debbie Trott Pierce

The Worship of God

Christmas Eve

Prelude   Wellman

Sing We Now of Christmas

Call to Worship

Leader:	People, look east!
People:	**Love the Lord is on the way.**
Leader:	The period of waiting is over! Behold, your Lord comes as an infant to you.
People:	**God comes as a child, so that we as children can go to God.**
Leader:	The Lord of the universe is a baby in a manger.
People:	**Mysteries and wonders of eternity and time, the one who spoke the world into being cries in his mother's arms.**
Leader:	Let us draw near and bow down.
People:	**O come, let us adore him.**
Leader:	Christ, the Lord.

Opening Hymn   Shaw

People, Look East

Christmas Eve Invocation (unison)

O God, who in your coming found that the world you had made had gone astray, make us anew and help us love you. Like little children ourselves, we are in awe of this night when our Lord came to us. Like little children, then, we come to you and worship you, our Lord and our Redeemer. Emmanuel, God with us, you are all we need. Stay with us, Lord Jesus, 'till morning is nigh. Amen.

Love the Lord is promised.

The First Lesson	Genesis 3:14-15
The Second Lesson	Isaiah 45:18-25
Carol	Wesley

Hark! The Herald Angels Sing

Love the Lord is announced.

The Third Lesson	Luke 1:57, 67-69
The Fourth Lesson	Luke 1:26-38
Carol	Rossetti

In the Bleak Midwinter

An Antiphonal Reading

"The Magnificat"
(based on Mary's Song)

Leader: We are here, the servants of the Lord. Let it be with us according to God's word.

People: Our souls will magnify the Lord, and our spirits rejoice in God our Saviour.

Women: For God has looked with favor on us, God's servants.

Men: For God has done great things for us, the blessed ones.

All: Holy be the name of the Lord!

Leader: Mercy is upon those who fear and reverence God, from generation to generation.

People: God has revealed great strength; God has scattered the proud and lifted the lowly.

Leader: God has fed the hungry.

People: The Lord has helped us and remembered us with mercy.

Leader: So it was promised to Adam and Eve.

People: So it is true for us today.

All: And it will be forever, Amen.

Love the Lord is near.

Carol	Brooks

O Little Town of Bethlehem

The Fifth Lesson	Matthew 1:18-24
The Sixth Lesson	Luke 2:1-7
Instrumental Interlude	Murray

Away in a Manger

The Lighting of the Christ Candle
The Seventh Lesson   Luke 2:8-20
Carol   English Carol

The First Noel

Love the Lord is here!
The Mystery of Communion

Leader:	The Lord be with you.
People:	**And also with you.**
Leader:	Christ the Lord is here—born in Bethlehem, born again in our hearts.
People:	**He is Lord of Lords and King of Kings—Jesus Christ, the first and last.**
Leader:	Lift up your hearts.
People:	**We lift them up unto the Lord.**
Leader:	It is right and a good and joyful thing always and everywhere to offer thanks to you God Almighty, Creator and Lover of heaven and earth, who in the quiet of the night in Bethlehem loved this world and gave your son for its salvation. Therefore, we praise you, welcoming love and joining our voices with the voices of angels and archangels and all the company of heaven to proclaim your holy name.
All:	**Holy, holy, holy Lord, God of power and might, heaven and earth are full of glory. Hosanna in the highest. Blessed is he who comes in the name of the Lord. Hosanna in the highest.**
Leader:	Holy and gracious God, in your infinite love you made us for yourself; and when we had fallen into sin and became subject to evil and death, you in your mercy sent Jesus Christ, your only eternal Son, to share our human nature, to live and die as one of us, to reconcile us to you the God and Lord of all. He was born of the virgin Mary, lived and died, stretching out his arms on the cross and offering himself as a perfect sacrifice for the world. On

41

the night he was handed over to suffering and death, he took bread. And when he had given thanks to you, he broke it and gave it to his disciples and said, "Take, eat. This is my body, given for you. Do this in remembrance of me." After supper he took the cup, and when he had given thanks to you, he gave it to them and said, "Drink this, all of you. This is my blood of the new covenant, which is shed for you and for many for the forgiveness of sins. Whenever you drink it, do this in remembrance of me." Therefore, together we can proclaim the mystery of faith:

All: **Christ has died. Christ is risen. Christ will come again.**

Leader: And now as our Savior Christ has taught us, we are bold to say:

All: **Our Father who art in heaven, hallowed be thy name. Thy kingdom come, thy will be done, on earth as it is in heaven. Give us this day our daily bread; and forgive us our trespasses as we forgive those who tresspass against us. And lead us not into temptation, but deliver us from evil. For thine is the kingdom and the power and the glory, forever. Amen.**

All: **Alleluia! Christ our Passover is sacrificed for us. Let us keep the feast. Alleluia.**

The Celebration of Communion

(Worshipers are invited to come forward as directed and kneel to receive Communion.)

The Eighth Lesson   Revelation 21:1-4; 22:12-24, 16-17, 20

Musical Offering   Manz
To Shepherds As They Watched by Night

Prayer

*The Passing of the Christmas Light
Alleluia

42

A Period of Silence

*Closing Carol   Gruber
Silent Night, Holy Night

Benediction (unison)
   Tonight for the first time, again,
   The prison gates are open.
   Music and sudden light
   Have interrupted our routine
   And swept the filth of habit from our hearts.
   O Lord, here and now our endless journey starts.
   Thanks be to God. Amen.

Postlude   German Folk Tune
Good Christian Saints, Rejoice

*Congregation Standing

Sermons

Children

The First Sunday of Advent
Love the Guest Is on the Way

We have changed the sanctuary for this special time in the church year. What have you noticed that is different? [The color purple, the Advent wreath, the banner, etc.] The color purple is the color of waiting and getting ready. It reminds us that we are getting ready and waiting for God to come, for the birth of Jesus.

The Advent wreath, with its four purple candles and one white candle, helps us count the Sundays until Jesus' birth. We won't light the white candle until midnight on Christmas Eve. The purple candle we light today is the first one, that of Love the Guest.

How do you get ready for a guest to come to your house? [clean up, prepare a meal, plan entertainment] The one coming at Christmas is God. Therefore, we must clean up our hearts, get ready to celebrate, and plan things to do so that Christmas is not just Santa and new toys, but rather a time of thinking about the baby Jesus and the love God showed in sending Jesus. Let's pray.

Dear Loving God, thank you for coming as the baby Jesus to show us how much you love us. Help us get ready in our hearts for your coming again. Amen.

The Second Sunday of Advent
Love the Rose Is on the Way

Now the sanctuary is different, even more so than last Sunday [previous Sunday night was the hanging of the green]. It looks like we are getting our sanctuary ready for a special guest. What do you see that shows we are getting ready and waiting? [purple stoles, purple banner, purple candles in the wreath and windows, purple bows on wreaths in the windows] The color purple is the color of getting ready and waiting.

For what are we getting ready? [The baby Jesus is coming, the birth of God, God with us] What helps us count the Sundays until Christmas? [The Advent wreath and the purple candles] Today we light the second purple candle, and we see there are only two more Sundays before Christmas. Last week we lit the candle for Love the Guest; this candle is the one for Love the Rose [display a rose in one hand].

A rose is a beautiful flower, but it is one that requires tender care, good soil, water, and sun. If a rose were to bloom in winter, it would be very special. If God were to come visit us this Christmas, or even today, it would be very special. Let's pray.

> *Loving God, help us prepare for your coming, getting ourselves ready and looking for you to appear. Amen.*

The Third Sunday of Advent
Love the Bird Is on the Way

The sanctuary looks ready for the baby Jesus to be born, for God to come this Advent season. The color purple is everywhere, reminding us to get ready and wait for God to come. That is what the word Advent means, "Coming."

What helps us count the Sundays until God comes? [the Advent wreath] Today we light the third purple candle. There is one more Sunday until Christmas. We have lit the candles for Love the Guest, Love the Rose, and this morning we light the candle for Love the Bird [display a bird cage].

Tell me, is a bird in a cage still a bird? What is a bird? A dictionary will tell us that a bird is an animal made for flying. It has wings and light bones and feathers and the ability to fly. Keeping it in a cage makes it hard for a bird to do what it should do, what it is born to do—fly. It should be free to be truly a bird. Maybe in the same way God is like the bird.

To prepare for God's coming, we must be ready for anything God wants to do. We must let God work freely in our lives, in our homes, and in our church, and then God will truly be God. Let's pray.

Loving God, we want you to come, so help us welcome you freely to do whatever you will in us. Amen.

The Fourth Sunday of Advent

Love the Star Is on the Way

It is our last Sunday before Christmas, so today we light the fourth purple candle on our Advent wreath. Do you remember what the color purple tells us? [It is time to get ready and wait] For what are we getting ready? [for the baby Jesus to be born, for God to come] I hope you've been getting ready by thinking about this wonderful gift God gave us, God with us in the coming of the baby Jesus.

We have lit the candles of Love the Guest, Love the Rose, Love the Bird, and today Love the Star [display a star ornament or a picture of a star]. Now the star is something you expect to see at Christmastime. What does a star do? [shines, gives off light, can tell us the direction to go] When Jesus came, people thought the things he did and said were so wonderful, they asked him who he was. He told them, "I am the light of the world."

When we are in a dark room, light helps us to see better. When God comes, we all see better what is important, where we are going, and what we ought to do. Jesus said he would never leave us. So at Christmas we celebrate a mystery. Jesus is the light that never leaves, and yet we look for it again and again. Let's pray.

Loving God, come, O come, and be the light before us and behind us and in us always. Amen.

Adults

The First Sunday of Advent
Love the Guest Is on the Way

Isaiah 40:3-11; Matthew 25:31-46; Ephesians 2:11-22

I'm sure all of you have things to do to get ready for "company." I'm probably not much different from you. My responsibility is to pick up, clean up, hang up, and cram in. You probably have to do the same thing. The biggest job is picking all that popcorn out from under the cushions of my favorite chair. All this just to get ready for guests.

Hospitality seems to have a harder time now than when I was younger. When I was a child, people would drop by our home and most likely stay for a meal and maybe all night. I had been in the ministry for ten years and in a lot of churches before I ever stayed in a motel. We just assumed we would be in a home. In the early years of our marriage we might wake up with sleeping bags all over the house. Sometimes we didn't know who was in them or how many. One of my big mistakes was inviting Ben to "come by any time." He did and stayed for a month. He almost broke up our marriage because he wanted to do all the cooking.

Hospitality is that wonderful gift of welcoming the stranger. The nomadic people of the biblical world could not have survived without it. The Greeks came to rank injustice to foreigners and strangers as an evil exceeded only by godlessness and lack of reverence for parents. God's people were strangers in Palestine, but they could never quite settle on what to do with the strangers in their midst. For most of the ancient world, the stranger was an enemy—an unknown sinister one who needed to be driven away. Yet, they were not quite sure because the stranger might be a messenger from God. This feeling of fear and suspicion was mixed with fascination, curiosity, and the need to be helpful. A story by Garrison Keillor tells it well.

A man is hijacked on the highway, robbed, beaten, stripped of all his clothing, and left stranded in the middle of the road in the middle of the night. He wonders through the woods, dazed and cold, and then

51

stumbles across a house where two ladies live. He knocks on the door, and the two women peer out at him from an upstairs window. One says to the other, "My soul, we can't let him in. He has no clothes." The other replies, "O, my goodness, we have to let the poor man in. He has no clothes."

In spite of fear and suspicion, biblical people approached each day with the expectation that the events of the day might contain messages addressed to them personally—omens, epiphanies, blessings, and teachers who would knowingly or unknowingly speak a message from the spiritual world. Jesus saw this clearly. "Just as you did it to one of the least of these who are members of my family, you did it to me" (Matt 25:40). His whole ministry was dependent on the hospitality of the people. He sent out disciples expecting hospitality in towns and villages (Matt 10:11: Luke 10:5).

How can we forget Abraham's gestures of hospitality in Genesis 18? From the door of his tent "looking east," he sees three figures coming toward him through the heat of the day. They look like ordinary people. Abraham runs out to meet them. There are gestures of welcoming, bowing before them, and a rather long speech, suggesting some anxiety on Abraham's part. He offers rest, water, and food. These "ordinary" strangers bring the promise that Isaac will be born, a reward beyond Sarah and Abraham's comprehension. Surely the writer of Hebrews had this story in mind. "Do not neglect to show hospitality to strangers, for by doing that some have entertained angels without knowing it" (13:2)

The Bible wants us to know that welcoming a stranger brings us close to an experience with God. It's a long way from Genesis 18 to Matthew 25, but we get a glimpse of Christ in the stranger. "I was a stranger, and you welcomed me."

With all this in the background it is not surprising that we make elaborate preparations during the Christmas season. Our hymn says it well: "Make your house fair as you are able/Trim the hearth and set the table."

"Have you done your decorating for Christmas?" means "Are you ready to welcome Christ into your home during the Christmas season?" But Christ is no stranger, we say. This is gentle Jesus meek and mild. This well-mannered, polite one will be welcomed into our home. He will not make waves. His name is on our tongues. He is "one of the family." He is one of us. Is that the way we see him?

Let's smooth out the rough edges and play down the contradictions. Let's not remind ourselves that he was seen as a glutton and a drunkard, a friend of tax collectors and sinners. Let's not recall that foxes and birds have holes and nests, but the Son of Man has no place to lay his head. Let's forget that he came into the world and the world knew him not. He came unto his own, but his own did not know him. Let's ignore the fact that he really was a stranger.

He was born in the same way we all were and would create chaos in your house just like any child would do. He got lost in the city and worried his parents to death most of the time. John baptized him and wondered if he got the right one. He was a stranger, alright—to his disciples, best friends, mother, brothers, sisters, and enemies. The disciples were scared of him. He taught in a way no one understood. In free obedience he did and said what only a person could do and say who was wholly surrendered to the will of God. And in the end they did him in—and it wasn't pretty. In fact, it was ugly and worse than any of us could ever imagine. Now, is that the kind of person you want in your house?

It's not that we aren't looking for a Messiah at Christmas. It's just that he isn't ever what we are looking for. He will always be a stranger in our midst. But being a stranger does not mean he is distant and unapproachable. This is a stranger who is full of wonder, one who fills our lives with amazement and astonishment, one who is beyond our understanding.

John Donne entered his pulpit in St. Paul's Cathedral in London on Christmas Day 1626, and began his sermon this way:

> Others die as martyrs, but Christ was born a martyr. He found Golgatha (where he was crucified) even in Bethlehem where he was born. For to his tenderness then, even the straws were almost as sharp as the thorns after, and the manger as uneasy at first as his cross at last. His birth and his death were but one continual act, and his Christmas Day and his Good Friday are but the evening and the morning of one and the same day.

The strange one, one whom we feel more comfortable with at a distance, now comes as a guest to the communion table. Is that the way it is? Do we invite him to this table? No, this stranger is not a guest; this stranger is the host. It's as if a stranger, a foreigner, comes into our house and suddenly becomes the master of ceremonies. We don't invite him to the table. It is his table, and he invites us. This is not my table, not our church's table, not the worship committee's table—although they have set it—not the deacons' or elders' table—although they will serve it. Christ the stranger invites, "Come, sit at the table, and be my guest."

The Second Sunday of Advent
Love the Rose Is on the Way

Isaiah 35:1-10; Matthew 13:24-30; 2 Corinthians 2:14-17

I'm not an expert on growing roses, but I do know that roses drench your senses with exquisite smells. Smells are close to our long-term memory and surer than sights and sounds to play on the heartstrings.

Roses have captivated and attracted people more than any other flower. They are strewn around at public ceremonies and banquets. Rose petals are used as pillow stuffings, and garlands of roses are used in the hair, for medicine, and for love potions. When Cleopatra welcomed Mark Anthony into her bedroom, the floor was covered in a foot and a half of rose petals. And so, the old saying, "Life really is a bed of roses." Diane Ackerman talks of a rose with an almost human complexion and mood, depending on the moisture and light of the day. It was appropriately named the "peace" rose in commemoration of May 2, 1945, the day Berlin fell to the Allied forces. There is no flower that triggers the imagination like the rose.

Let's allow our imaginations to run across the Mediterranean, along the coastal line just south of Mount Carmel to a plain called the Plain of Sharon, a fifty-mile stretch of land with abundant marshes and forests. Sharon was a pastureland for flocks and a place for herds to lie down as people sought after a living God. On this plain a flower bloomed profusely in spring and autumn. It was a wildflower, an original, not a hybrid.

Sharon was a tableland lush with vegetation, a place of fertile growth in a desert land. Surely the imagination of Isaiah was fired by the Plain of Sharon. It became a familiar theme with him. The new growth in nature will signal an important religious, cultural, and political event. The natural world and social/relational world will blend and throw light on each other. A well-known daily reality will open doors to a new reality. This new day will begin down at the root of things, working in the earth. Like the rose that grows on the Plain of Sharon, a time will come when water will flow in the wilderness. Thorns will be replaced by flowers. God will make the deserts like Eden and the wastelands like the

55

garden of the Lord. Joy and gladness will be found with thanksgiving, and the sounds of singing will be in the air. People will flourish like a spring of water. The wilderness and the solitary place will be glad, and the desert will rejoice and blossom.

How shall it blossom? Like a rose! Beside these rushing streams and blossoming roses in the desert can be seen a highway, a pilgrim's way. The ransomed people of the Lord who crowd that highway will sing with incredulous joy. God has opened up a new and living way. My soul, all this from reflecting on a rose?

Isaiah wants us to look at essence, at the root of things. Where there is root, there is hope for a new beginning. This is a rose that will grow anywhere, as Isaiah says, "like a root out of dry ground" (53:2). Down at the root of things is where Jesus Christ moved all of his life—the undetected sickness, the buried sin, the repressed experience, the ignored holiness. Jesus was "subterranean," working at the nerve endings. He was the true root (*radix*—"radical"), reminding the church of his true nature. "It is I, Jesus. . . . I am the root" (Rev 22:16).

The rose was a wild one, not hybridized. When you find a rose in bloom, you know there has never been another one like it, and there will never be one like it again. Sometimes you can look at a flower, and it will reenergize your sense of wonder at being alive. You'll lose your cynicism that comes from living in a world where everything seems to have utilitarian value. What good is it? When you start asking this question, you are not far from wondering what good are you or the person sitting next to you. What good is a rose? Not much use that we know about, but somehow a rose gives the sense of being alive and why it's worth being alive.

David Adam, attending to a rose cut fresh from the bush, suddenly became aware of its beauty. He commented in *The Cry of the Deer*,

> There it stood with the mystery of life in it, and many of the mysteries of the universe; and it had presented itself to me. I was captured for awhile by this "mystery to be enjoyed." But even more, under my very gaze, a Presence had invaded my little world. The only thing that kept Him out had been my inability to see. Now, "the Lord is in this place," and I knew it.

This is the knowledge that restores wholeness to everyday life, that awakens us to the vital link between God and all we lost when we left that first garden, our true home. It is this knowledge that gives us a foretaste of harmony that will embrace everything that exists.

"Down at the root of things" reminds us that God is always active although sometimes hidden. God does not leave us to our own dealings until suddenly deciding that we can't make it on our own. Finally, when we are at our breaking point, God arrives. God is not sometimes present and sometimes absent. God is always present and sometimes hidden.

Suppose we could show you a handwoven tapestry with a background of lush, thick vegetation. Scattered in this vast expanse are small rose buds not yet in full bloom. In contrast to the dominant threads of the fabric, the patterns of the small rose buds are scattered secondary designs. To see the true design, however, we would have to turn the tapestry over and see the intricate weaving on the backside that created the design on the top side. The underside is predominantly the threads of the small buds unbroken, moving from one bud to the other. In the center is one bud blossomed to full flower. In this full blossom we see all the subtle revealings of the others. The central brilliant blossom enables us to see the possibilities of all the others.

To see God at work, we have to turn history over and look at the underside, revealing what God has been doing all the time. God is revealed fully in the one rose that bloomed fully for a short moment and "wasted its fragrance in the desert air" of an obscure land called Palestine.

I remember a visit to John and Dele Wilson's home in Nashville, Tennessee. We were invited to their home one Wednesday evening to observe a "night-blooming cactus." I remember making a snide remark to a friend: "I can't believe I'm going to sit around for an hour or two, waiting for a flower to bloom." But we did, and I joked, made side comments, and the food was good. And then, suddenly, it happened. The cactus quickly opened into full flower right before our eyes. Fifteen or twenty people were sitting there in stunned silence, tears coming to their eyes. One person, sitting over in a corner, sobbed quietly. In thirty minutes it wilted, leaving a fragrance in the air that made us heady, almost drunk with the power of it.

This one, this Rose of Sharon, was old before his time. He took root, down at the nerve endings, and the world did its work on him. He came to full flower and was gone quickly, leaving the fragrance and smell of his life all around us. And then, suddenly, without warning, he blossomed forth in us.

The Third Sunday of Advent
Love the Bird Is on the Way

Deuteronomy 32:7-12; Malachi 3:16, 4:2; Luke 13:31-34

In my memory there are three indelible experiences with birds. The first is from college. My roommate during my first semester had a bird. Now, when I was asking the usual questions to ascertain our compatibility, it did not occur to me to inquire of her: "Will you be bringing a bird?" She did, and in less than two weeks everything I owned—every article of clothing, every suitcase, every book, every drawer, all my make-up—was littered with bird seed. The small room we shared was no place for a bird, and I confess there was little genuine sorrow on my part when the bird died later in the semester.

My second experience was in Guston, Kentucky, in the home of one of the members of my husband's first pastorate. The bird belonged to Ruth Butler. Ruth was a round-the-clock caregiver of her husband Earl who suffered from a degenerative muscle disease. Earl was completely immobile, lived in a hospital bed in their living room, was fed through a tube, had an oxygen tank at the ready, and could only communicate by what appeared to me mere flickers of his eyes—which Ruth would interpret.

Ruth was an unusual woman to find in rural Kentucky. She was well-read, well-traveled, an engaging conversationalist, delightful company, uncomplaining, and devoted to her husband. As far as we knew, she only left her husband's side to go to the doctor or to walk to the corner for some new books from the library bookmobile. Whenever we visited Ruth and Earl, sometime during the visit Ruth would walk across the room and ceremoniously let her bird out of the cage. The bird would swoop around the room and dive-bomb over our heads and occasionally perch on Ruth's head or shoulders. It seemed to give Ruth such pleasure to see this bird fly free in her living room.

My third experience was at the aviary of the Memphis Zoo one summer with my husband and children. We happened upon a bird trainer training a magnificent falcon. It had a hood over its eyes and was tethered to a leash in order to guide its flight from one perch to another. This bird, born with the capacity to soar and swoop and glide and hunt, was made to fly and strain against its tether, held to a particular height and no more, a particular distance and no more. I confess I know little about birds and less about falconry, but I was mesmerized and rather saddened to see such a beautiful creature straining against a rope and flying in such an awkward fashion.

A bird is a wonder of creation. Gerard Manly Hopkins' poem evokes so well the majesty of a bird in flight, a bird being what it was designed to be . . . "brute beauty and valour and act, oh, air, pride, plume." According to the *Audubon Society Encyclopedia of Animal Life,*

> There are approximately 9,000 species of birds, and their adaptability and mobility have permitted them to reach every portion of the world, including the most remote oceans, the frozen vastness of the Antarctic, the depths of deep caves, the top slopes of the Himalayas, the mud bottom 200 feet below the surface of the sea, and the darkest recesses of the jungle. Their ability to fly still mystifies us, though we can find our way through space to the moon.

Birds are a mystery to us. From Icarus and Daedalus to the Wright Brothers to the new Boeing 737, we have tried to mimic their power and independence and their singular attribute: they fly . . . naturally. And a bird is free. Marvelously so.

I heard of a bird exhibition at a football game at the Air Force Academy in Colorado Springs, Colorado. During half-time, falconers set free a group of falcons. These falcons would go up above the stadium, soar around, and then return to their trainers' arms. One bird in particular went up, soared, and came down; went up a second time, soared, and came down; went up a third time, soared and soared and soared . . . gone, never to return. An embarrassed stadium announcer could only say, "They do that sometimes folks!"

Birds are unpredictable. Birds will be free. Think about it. We have fences for dogs, leashes and collars for most pets. But to keep a bird, we must have it in a cage. We hood and tether it. We clip its wings. But it will be free if it is to be . . . a bird.

So Love the Bird is on the way. Our hymn speaks of God coming to inhabit the nest of our hearts and our beings and coming unexpectedly, long after the nest is prepared; of then teaching us to fly, to try out our wings even when circumstances have "frozen" them. The poem presents the poet's glimpse of a transcendent moment of watching a bird, specifically a windhover, fly steady in the face of swirling winds. Such a moment was for this poet like witnessing Christ's passion, crucifixion, and resurrection. He sees it likewise in newly plowed earth and burning embers. He sees it all around—a world crammed full of God—God appearing, God coming, and God speaking.

The Scriptures present to us three visions of Love the Bird. God is as a mother eagle caring for her people Israel, nesting, hovering, spreading her wings over them, bearing them up, guiding them. The prophet Malachi sees a judgment day in which God as a sunbird will rise and spread healing wings over all who trust in the Lord. In Luke, Jesus identifies himself as a mother hen who would gather an obstinate brood in for safety and protection and even for nurturing comfort, but is refused. There are other images of birds in the Bible: the dove, which symbolizes innocence and the pure Holy Spirit of God; the quail, which provided for the needs of the Israelites in the wilderness; the raven, which for Elijah served as a symbol of God's love for His servant and of God's sovereignty over nature; the sparrow, whose meekness and seeming insignificance recalls God's care for all creation.

But the image of God, of Christ coming, does not fit neatly with my understanding of a bird. A bird on the wing is glorious. A bird feeding its young is endearing. A bird preparing its nest for the eggs it or its mate will lay is a marvel. "How do they know? Who tells them it is time?" But a bird in the hand, a bird flying nearby, or a bird in our house is frightening and unsettling. We marvel; we are amazed; we run for cover; we shoo it away or grab the broom and chase it out the door. So what can this mean?

Christ is coming. Love the Bird is on the way. Not very comforting unless you are a bird. Maybe that is the rub. We fear we can't recognize God or see God or hear God or even want to because, like a bird, God is so very Other. Will we recognize God? Will we embrace the holy moment of Christ's coming during this Advent season? "Meek and mild, he became a little child." Our attempts at merrymaking and recapturing that kind of childlike joy and excitement seem childish or forced, or worse, false. "My peace I give to you. . . . Peace I leave with you. . . . peace that endures." For many of us, we can no more stop the racing of our minds than we can stop the beating of our hearts. "Rest for your souls. Easy burdens and light loads." We sleep, we rest only if we are exhausted and then still awaken tired. "Love one another, because love is from God; everyone who loves is born of God and knows God" (1 John 4:7). As a tired young child once said, "Sometimes I just can't like anybody."

Christ came in such an unexpected form to such a hostile world. What could this baby do being born into a world at war? And Christ comes daily, moment by moment to you and me. But given the option of taking off our shoes at the burning bush and hearing the still small voice, we wander off to pick blackberries or turn up the volume on the television set. God appears in epiphanal moments—a bird, a cactus rose unfolding, a burning ember, a star, shining eyes, a lump in the throat, love spoken, kindness given, a touch, a tear, the spiritual insight of a child.

Too often we receive such moments of God's appearing as we would a bird in the house. We shoo it out or lock it up or open the door or window, hoping it will vanish before it changes us. We do not for one moment wonder. For too many of us, a bird is too dangerous to let fly free, unless, like my friend Ruth Butler, our lives are aching to be upset, to be turned over, to be set free.

Gerard Manley Hopkins' image of Christ is "a billion times told lovelier, more dangerous." God in the house, God living free in our lives speaking to all our moments is *dangerous*. It seems that God does not belong there because God shakes things up; makes us look in the mirror; asks us to be emotionally there for people who irritate us, to forgive, to include, to risk being excluded or rejected or refused, to be reconciled, to celebrate what is now and stop regretting the past or wishing for the future.

If Jesus came into our homes, would he sweep away the tree and the lights and the glitter and all the gifts? Would he, in temple-cleansing fashion, so clean out our homes of the trappings of Christmas? And leave—what? the plastic manger scene in the corner? Or, is even that so infused with our imaginations and Americanizations that he would toss it out, too? I suppose what would be left would be people; just folks, just the people in our lives—mother, father, sons, daughters, sisters, brothers, aunts, uncles, friends, co-workers, neighbors, church folks. God is not interested in inhabiting a manger, a nest, a tree, a cage, or a box. God is interested in coming to be in us, in you, in me. And we will never be the same again if God so comes.

But we want a baby not a bird. We want the table set, not overturned. We want the fresh anticipation and pure joy of Christmas that our children exhibit, but we want everything back in its place by New Year's Day. The more secure we are with our place in the world, with things as they are, the less comfortable we are with the metaphor of God as a bird.

Our friend Ruth Butler, weary with the world, opened the bird's cage and embraced its dangerous flight. It flew in her living room. It flew in her kitchen. The fluttering of bird's wings mimicked her own heart stirring to be free, to be saved from the monotony, the burden of her life.

And so if Christ coming into the world does not scare the dickens out of us, there is something terribly wrong. We have packaged and planned and sterilized God's coming that even a stinking stable smells sweet. Herod knew enough to be scared; he knew that God's coming was going to shake things up, like God always does when God comes. But not us, for we have made it sweet and clean and oh so manageable.

Being a Christian at Christmas is as nearly impossible as Kierkegaard said that being a Christian in Christendom is. Being a Christian at Christmas means embracing the wild side of Jesus that is shaking the foundations of this world, of your world, for the Christ who comes is a wild thing we cannot harness or tether or cage or control. It is God, Almighty God bursting free of a teenager's womb and hurtling into the hurly burly tumble of human existence where children die and somebody always loses and God flies the high wind to the terrible cross. Like a bird, God is coming. Look there, Christ the Free, Wild Bird comes . . . to you . . . for you. Amen.

The Fourth Sunday of Advent

Love the Star Is on the Way

Isaiah 9:2-7; John 1:1-14; Revelation 1:9-20; 22:16

Suppose God took all the constellations of stars, added a little more sparkle, shuffled them around a bit, and decided to provide a little show. We would walk out in the night, look up into the night sky, and there it would be, written boldly in the eastern sky. "Hey, it's me! I really exist." Maybe a moon to dot the "I," a meteor for a comma, and a comet for an exclamation point if God thought they were needed.

How would people respond? How would you respond? Some would sink to their knees on the spot. Some would shout and dance, running to get their cameras. Some would be scared out of their wits and try to find some place to hide. Some would be struck with awe and terror. Others would yawn and go about their business, thinking the whole thing was another promotional stunt. The artistic among us would go crazy. There would be tears of regret: "If I had only known, I would have lived differently." There would be a jolt of hope for the sick and afflicted. All people of faith would get a sudden surge of smug confidence, knowing we had been right all along, even more right than we ever dreamed. We couldn't get all the people in church. We would have to run church on the hour every day for weeks. We would kick ourselves for not getting that new sanctuary built. Wars would cease; crime would stop; people would reconcile. A peaceful quiet would fall over the world.

Every night there it would be, visibly shouting at us from the heavens, sometimes in different scripts, in different languages, in different colors. There would be a million sermons entitled "Hey, It's Me!"—maybe some choruses and anthems. It would be all we ever wanted, or would it?

Like everything else, this revelation would become common. Even though it would continue for centuries to come, no matter how God presented it, the display just wouldn't make any difference anymore. Somehow we need more. It's simply not enough that God is up there in the night. We need God right here in the day—not that God is out there in the cold brightness of the stars. God is right here in the thick of our day and mixing it up with us in the muck, misery, madness, and marvel of our lives. That is the miracle we are looking for and the miracle we get. Not just starlight, starbright in the middle of the night, but God walking with us in the helter skelter of the day. A manifestation, or epiphany, of God in the night skies will not impress us very much and for very long.

Not so with biblical people. The night skies reflected the activity of the cosmos. The heavens declared the glory of God, and the firmament showed God's handiwork. God led the people with a cloud by day and a pillar of fire by night. The heavens were full of the activity of God. From the beginning God hung the great lights in the heavens. To find out what God was doing, you had to look beyond the earth and "up" into the sky. Isaiah and Ezekiel warned the people that God's judgment would come on the earth when God made the stars dark. The stars would fall, the hosts of heaven would rot away, and the sky would roll up like a scroll.

Since God creates light and darkness, God is Lord of the darkness, and God is able to turn even darkness into light. God makes the world bright in order for us to see, not only to orient us to objects, but to help us understand ourselves in the world. That is the reason we do not grope in darkness and are able to see our way. Scripture proclaims that light shines in the darkness. But recognizing that light shines in the darkness is not enough. We must turn toward it and walk in it and not be mere admirers of it.

The sky is the one visual constant in our lives, a complex backdrop of every venture, thought, and emotion. Although we tend to think of it as invisible, our ancestors looked at it with fear and wonder, a roof of changing moods and colors, somehow the resting place of all their loved ones, where choirs of angels sang. Throughout time people have looked up to figure out where they were and often who they were. Wanderers waited till the night to find their way home, hoping the lights in the heavens would help them find their way.

Second Peter gives us the admonition to pay attention. "Be attentive to this as to a lamp shining in a dark place, until the day dawns and the morning star rises in your hearts" (1:19). This is the star that precedes the dawn, the bringer of morning. This star, coming out of Jacob, fills us with marvelous light, the radiance of the divine glory shining in our hearts.

So Peter, look east. A star is rising, pushing away darkness, introducing the dawning of a new age. This event is God's doing. The light has not yet arrived; its time has not yet come. But it's on the way, and we await with fear and joy. When the light finally breaks in the east signaling the new day and the new age, the world will be seen in a new way. What is will disappear into what was. What we all have hoped for will appear into what can be. The old ones will see and be born again. The little ones will speak with the wisdom of the old ones. The first will be last and the last first. The high will be low and the low high. Up will be down, and down will be up. Morning comes. The day is at hand.

The morning hours have always been significant for me. As a 9-year-old, I woke with a start at 4:00 A.M. and walked into a bedroom where 4 neighborhood women were sitting. My grandmother had just died. At almost the same hour 26 years later my mother died after a courageous 23-year battle with cancer. My sister and I walked out of the hospital in Erie, Pennsylvania, into a bitter cold winter night. My eyes were drawn to the eastern sky. There it was, the morning star. I remember the first words I said to my sister: "Well, it's a new day for Mom."

There's something about the morning hours, significant experiences between midnight and dawn. I remember the morning when my daughter and I became friends. It was the summer before her senior year in high school, driving across West Texas with the rest of the kids in the van asleep. She knew my weird sleep habits, and so we talked for long hours —significant talking, and maybe for the first time. There have been other nights of pushing away the darkness around and in front, looking for light. This morning I awoke early, slipped into clothes, and came to sit at the back of the church, looking east. It was a breezy morning, with changing pink and purple, yellow and orange clouds. The first light came shining on our youth and children's buildings, appropriately signaling the locations of our new day.

In *An Experience Named Spirit*, John Shea narrates an event in the life of Michael Mulligan. After his retirement from Sears he decided to take his 12-year-old granddaughter to Ireland, his home, to meet a brother whom he had not seen for 40 years. He was the second of 4 sons and 3 daughters. Jerry, the oldest son, received the family blessing, and along with the blessing, the family farm. There was nothing to do but move along. Michael threw his shoes across his shoulder to save wear and tear, walked barefoot over the mountain, and caught a boat to America. The year was 1908. Every year he sent a letter and a check to his brother. "Not much new here," he said in the brief letter. After the turn of the year, a return letter arrived from his brother. "Not much new here, either." The checks were never mentioned.

But in June 1948, he wrote a letter out of season. "We are bringing our granddaughter for a visit to Ireland. Would you be home during the evening of July 11?" A return letter came the last of June. "I would. We will be expecting you for dinner." When they arrived on July 11, the stone-and-thatch cottage was much like he had remembered it 40 years earlier. The brothers met at the door with hands extended, but their eyes never met. Inside, the table was already set. The dinner was plain and good, the talk general, the kind of talk that wears one out. The night came; the talk slowed. The wives and granddaughters went to bed and slipped into sleep. The brothers sat at the table alone. "Are you a rich American?" "I am not." "Are you a rich Irish landowner?" "I am not."

The older brother stood, moved to the cabinet, reached for a large loaf of bread and a knife, and came back to the table. The younger brother moved to the back bedroom, slipped a hand into a suitcase, and brought out a bottle of bourbon whiskey he had brought from the States.

The first one up in the morning was the granddaughter. She slipped out of the bedroom and into the kitchen. There on the table were bread crumbs, a knife, and an empty bottle. The door of the cottage was open, and she looked out. The sun was beginning to climb in a clear sky and lit the field up to the house. In the middle of the field were the brothers inspecting the earth, like a mother checking a newborn baby. They must have been up all night, she thought to herself.

The brothers turned, saw her, and waved. And side by side, step by step, they came toward her. She now knew, although she had never stayed up all night to beat back the darkness, that when her time came, she could do it. And when they got within earshot, she shouted out to them, "O wow! You made it all the way to morning." Amen.

67

Educational Activities

Older Children

Unit Introduction
The colors and pageantry of this time of year can help children to experience visually some of the mystery of faith and especially to develop worship skills to deflect the overwhelming flood of commercial Christmas. The challenge is to teach children that these Advent themes are metaphorical ideas about God and God's coming. Christ, the face of God's love—coming in the form of a guest, a rose, a bird, and a star—is a vivid metaphor, but rich enough to be within the reach of older children. Advent is a time of preparation for all of us, far beyond the purchase of presents or decorating of trees. It is the setting aside of time

to read the Bethlehem story and to mark time with Christian symbols (the Advent wreath and candles) to build anticipation for Christmas that perhaps will present an alternative to anticipating presents.

Unit Project
Each child will make an Advent wreath for use in the home. The wreath and first candle will be assembled on the first Sunday, and a candle added each successive Sunday. The children will enjoy decorating their candles with interpretations of the metaphors: guest, rose, bird, and star. You may also choose to make candle cups in the shape of the different metaphors and place these on the wreath.

To Think About . . .

For session 1: Arrange the room furnishings in such a way as to demonstrate preparation for the coming of the children and a guest. Provide an adorned chair in which no one sits and an elaborate table setting before it. Invite as a guest speaker someone who works in a community clothes closet or food pantry, Meals-on-Wheels program, or prison ministry.

For session 2: Bring a small bouquet of roses or strong smelling flowers. Prepare opaque containers with about 10 strong smelling items (onion, perfume, mint, orange, coffee grounds, peanut butter, etc.)

For session 3: Display bird nests, bird eggs, bird cages, and bird pictures. Invite an expert on birds to give a short talk on birds, *or* prepare one yourself. Focus on how birds prepare nests and then care for their young and prepare them for flight. Show a short clip from the movie, *The Birds.* For memory verse time, make paper birds or origami cranes.

For session 4: Hang a star in a prominent location in the room. Secure biblical costumes, a manger with hay, and large and small candles for each child. Ask a student in the class who is a Boy Scout or Girl Scout, or someone who is familiar with stars, to share with the class about how to navigate by the stars.

The First Sunday of Advent
Love the Guest Is on the Way

Matthew 25:31-46

PREPARING FOR THE JOURNEY

Key Verse
The king will answer, "I tell you, just as you did it to one of the least of these who are members of my family, you did it to me." Matthew 25:40

Key Concept
The coming of Jesus at Christmas and his coming again require careful preparation, both physical and spiritual, which are enhanced by each other.

Educational Aims
To introduce the unit on Advent and the theme "Love Is on the Way"; to familiarize children with the Christian calendar; to enhance family worship by introducing the Advent wreath to one's family worship

Resources You Will Need

Stepping In
a liturgical Christian calendar marking all the special days and colors, 8"x11" sheets for the children to color and label the days and colors of the church year, crayons, colored pencils, markers.

Stepping Up
taped recording of "People, Look East" and printed words of stanza 1 and the refrain, a Bible for each child, appropriate pictures for the story

Retracing Your Steps
snack and drink for the children to serve each other; the worksheet "The Christian Year" (p. 77); supplies for making individual Advent wreaths:

greenery, circular styrofoam forms, purple candles and candle decorating supplies (soft colored wax, scissors, glue gun, glue sticks)

Stepping Beyond
Invite someone involved in community outreach (ex: prison ministry, Meals-On-Wheels, clothes closet, food pantry) to share with the children and perhaps suggest ways they can help.

Stepping Out
Christian year calendars, assembled wreaths, one candle per child

Before You Teach
Familiarize yourself with the church calendar and its significant dates and seasons. Prepare to tell the story of the sheep and the goats (Matt 25).

GUIDING THE JOURNEY

Stepping In
Purchase or prepare a poster-sized calendar of the Christian church year. Be sure it identifies such key events as Easter cycle, Christmas cycle, Eastertide, Lent, Epiphany, Advent, Ordinary Time, and the three special days: Easter, Christmas, and Pentecost.

As the children arrive, ask them to view the poster. Distribute coloring sheets similar to the poster for the children to label and color. Have available multiple sets of red, green, purple, and white (if not printed on white paper) crayons or markers or colored pencils. The children will later learn to explore the definitions of the terms in *Retracing Your Steps.*

Stepping Up
Play a recording of "People, Look East." Distribute song sheets of stanza 1 and the refrain. Sing the song together. Select a child to light the first candle of the class Advent wreath. Introduce the unit theme for the season of Advent. A brief explanation of metaphors and the use of them in the Bible may be helpful, especially those relating to Christ: Bread of Life, True Vine, Good Shepherd, Light, Water of Life, etc. Draw the children's attention to the empty chair and the place set before it.

Explain: The Scripture for this session presents Jesus as one who identifies with people who are in need and are outcasts. He comes as a guest and a stranger. We may be unaware of his presence. Jesus gives us the opportunity to serve and love him through service to others.

Ask the children to open their Bibles to Matthew 25:31-46. Assign 4 children to read the 4 different "voices" in the story: the narrator, the king, the righteous, and the accursed.

Storyteller's Questions
• When does this judgment occur?
• What kind of sin is condemned by the king?
• What services does the king commend?
• Who do you think are the least members in the king's family?
• What are some characteristics of the sheep and the goats?
• Who are some "strangers" through whom one can serve the king?

Retracing Your Steps
Provide a snack and let the children take turns serving each other "in Jesus name." Encourage them to identify the "needy strangers" they can serve in their school, church, neighborhood, family, etc.

Ask the children to assemble their Advent wreaths and decorate the first candle of Advent. Give each child a purple candle. Let them use soft colored wax to decorate the candle. For example, one candle could have a cup tipped over and pouring out blue water (giving a cup of cold water in Jesus' name). Let the children be creative in how they develop the metaphor of a guest or stranger.

Provide the children the opportunity to explore further the events and seasons of the liturgical year by completing the worksheet "The Christian Year."

Stepping Beyond
Older children enjoy helping those less fortunate, though they may feel shy initially. This lesson gives concrete examples of ways they may serve God through service to others. Brainstorm with the children ideas of service projects (ex: Make small gifts for hospitalized children or for nursing home patients who receive few visitors.)

Present a speaker who works with a community outreach project. Ask the guest to suggest ways the class can help in the ministry.

Stepping Out
Invite the children to share their activities and ideas about service projects. Pray that each one will anticipate the coming of Christ and look for ways to serve and love him through the guests who come into their lives.

The Christian Year

(I) Match the color (left) to the season of the Christian year it represents (right).

Green	Advent and Lent
Purple	Easter
Red	Ordinary time
White	Pentecost

(II) Match the season (left) of the Christian year to its description (right).

Advent	4 Sundays before Christmas
Christmas	6 Sundays after Easter
Christmastide	6 Sundays of preparing for Easter
Easter	Celebration of Jesus' birth
Eastertide	Celebration of Jesus' resurrection
Epiphany	Sundays after Christmas and before Epiphany
Lent	The day God gave the Holy Spirit to the Church
Ordinary Time	Time between Pentecost and Advent
Pentecost	Visit of the Wise Men to the young Jesus

The Second Sunday of Advent
Love the Rose Is on the Way

2 Corinthians 2:14-17

PREPARING FOR THE JOURNEY

Key Verse
But thanks be to God, who in Christ always leads us in triumphal procession, and through us spreads in every place the fragrance that comes from knowing him. 2 Corinthians 2:14

Key Concept
Paul's memories of ministry revealed to him the wonder of how God can use Christians in every circumstance as an "aroma of Christ."

Educational Aims
To learn more about the church year; to remember the year and opportunities of ministr; to examine what kind of influence we are and what kind of influence we can be

Resources You Will Need

Stepping In
vented and numbered opaque containers containing strong smelling items, paper, pencils

Stepping Up
taped recording of "People, Look East" and printed words of stanza 2 and the refrain, a Bible for each child

Retracing Your Steps
pencils, Bibles, art supplies (paper, markers, crayons), worksheet "Who Am I?" (p. 81)

Stepping Beyond
supplies for making individual Advent wreaths: greenery, circular styrofoam forms, candles, soft colored molding wax, scissors, glue gun/sticks

Stepping Out
second Advent candle

Before You Teach
Prepare to summarize the events Paul recorded in 2 Corinthians 1 and 2,
and 11:23-29. Read the focal passage, 2 Corinthians 2:14-17.

GUIDING THE JOURNEY

Stepping In
Distribute pencils and paper. Invite the children to the table where the
"smell test" will take place. Ask them to number 1-10 on their papers.
Instruct them to list beside each number what they smell in the container
with the same number. Offer a prize to the child who has the most correct answers. Ask each child to choose a smell they really like and one
they dislike.

Tell the children that during this session our focus is "Love the Rose
Is on the Way." They will read how Paul sees Christians as aromas or
strong smells of Christ in the world, pleasing to some and despised by
others.

Stepping Up
Play the recording of "People, Look East." Distribute song sheets of
stanza 2 and the refrain. Assign a child to light the second candle of the
class Advent wreath. Pray with the children in thankfulness for Jesus'
coming at Christmas and coming again someday in love for us.

Ask the children to open their Bibles to 2 Corinthians. Share that
today's memory verse is part of a passage in which Paul remembers some
highs and lows of his ministry, all within God's leading. Summarize the
experiences that led Paul to give thanks in 2 Corinthians 2:14-17. Examples are: comfort in times of trouble (vv. 3, 4, 5), hardships in Asia (v. 8),

a strong desire to be with this group of Christians (vv. 16-19), the anointing they received from God (vv. 21-22). Locate 2 Corinthians 11:23-29. Summarize the hardships Paul endured. Read the focal passage together.

Storyteller's Questions
• What is the aroma or fragrance of which Paul speaks?
• What kinds of people like the "fragrance"? Why?
• What kinds of people do not like the "fragrance"? Why?
• What does Paul mean when he asks, "Who is sufficient for these things?"—in other words, of being the smell of death and the smell of life to others?
• What is unique about the ministry of Paul and of those like him?
• Why do Paul and his friends share their faith so sincerely?

Retracing Your Steps
Distribute pencils and copies of the worksheet "Who Am I?" Ask the children to complete their worksheets, using their Bibles if needed. Discuss the influence/aroma of these different persons as the children respond to the worksheet.

Ask the children to draw their interpretations of what Paul meant when he said, "Through us [God] spreads in every place the fragrance that comes from knowing him" (2 Corinthians 2:14).

Stepping Beyond
Decorate candles. Assist newcomers in assembling their Advent wreaths. Encourage the children to decorate their second candle with a rose. Provide soft colored molding wax to attach to the purple candles.

Talk about how we are aromas of Christ wherever we go and how that can sometimes be difficult. Children at this age are aware of peer influence and can draw encouragement from each other in how to be strong in their faith and influence.

Stepping Out
In group time ask the children to share their interpretations of being "an aroma of Christ." Pray that they will continue to anticipate the coming of Christ and look for ways to reflect the aroma of Christ.

Who Am I?

I was sold into slavery by my brothers, but God used it for good to save them and all of Egypt from starvation. (Genesis 39–50)

_____

I lied to my father and cheated my brother, but God still blessed me and made me into a nation of believers. (Genesis 25–28)

_____

I was the only female judge and prophet in Israel. I went into battle with Barak to help deliver my people. (Judges 4)

_____

I was a very reluctant missionary who became fishbait. I finally made it to Ninevah to preach repentance to the people.

_____

I was a prostitute in Jericho who helped the spies from Israel and saved my family. (Joshua 2) _____

I was a faithful daughter-in-law whom God blessed. (Ruth 1–4)

_____

I have two names in the Bible. I was known for always doing good and helping the poor. Peter prayed for me when I died, and God brought me back to life. (Acts 9:36-41) _____

I was a very enthusiastic deacon in the early church. Paul witnessed and approved of my death by stoning. (Acts 7:54-60)

_____

The Third Sunday of Advent
Love the Bird Is on the Way

Luke 13:31-34

PREPARING FOR THE JOURNEY

Key Verse
How often have I desired to gather your children together as a hen gathers her brood under her wings, and you were not willing! Luke 13:34b

Key Concept
The coming of Jesus at Christmas and his coming again is of one who loves us and yet comes to us in unpredictable ways, asking us to live differently.

Educational Aims
To encourage children in spiritual anticipation of Christ's coming at Christmas and his coming again; to consider other metaphors in the Bible that help us see God better and teach us about God and God's love; to see how God's love calls for different responses from us

Resources You Will Need

Stepping In
bird nests, various sizes and colors of eggs, birdcages, a short segment of the movie *The Birds*

Stepping Up
taped recording of "People, Look East" and printed words of stanza 3 and the refrain, a Bible for each child, appropriate pictures for storytelling

Retracing Your Steps
worksheet "God Is Like . . ." (p. 86), Bibles, pencils, paper birds, clothesline, words of the key verse printed on 3"x5" cards

<u>Stepping Beyond</u>
supplies for making individual Advent wreaths: greenery, circular styrofoam forms, candles, soft colored molding wax, scissors, glue gun, glue sticks

<u>Stepping Out</u>
third candle for home Advent wreath

<u>Before You Teach</u>
Become familiar with Psalm 91 and Luke 13, which describe God as a nurturing bird and other images

GUIDING THE JOURNEY

Stepping In
Prepare a display of various bird-related items (nests, eggs of various sizes and colors, bird cages). Leave the bird cages open to build anticipation of a bird coming. A live bird may or may not prove more distracting than helpful, depending on the group (and the bird!). Have an empty clothesline in place. Let the children make an origami crane with paper, *or* before class make one for each of the words of the key verse and have them "perched" on the line.

As the children arrive, invite them to look at the items on the clothesline and/or make their origami cranes. Ask a birdwatcher or a teacher to present a short lecture about birds, particularly their nurturing traits, their nests, and how they prepare their young for flight.

Explain that the focus of this session is "Love the Bird Is on the Way." Refer to Luke 13:31-34 where Jesus uses the image of a mother hen to describe his love for Jerusalem, a people and city that rejected God's love repeatedly, and to Psalm 91 in which God's care and comfort are elaborated with the image of a bird.

Stepping Up
Play the recording of "People, Look East." Distribute song sheets for stanza 3 and the refrain. Sing the song together. Assign a child to light the third candle of the class Advent wreath.

Invite the children to open their Bibles to Psalm 91. Let each child read a verse or two. Encourage them to raise their hands when they hear something that suggests the image of a bird. Have them close their eyes and listen to another reading of the psalm, this time by one reader. Ask them to share the images in their minds.

Ask the children to turn to Luke 13:31-34. Ask a teacher or child to read this passage to the group as the group reads silently. Point out the similar image of the bird.

Storyteller's Questions
• What does the writer of Psalm 91 find in God?
• What does God seem to promise those who trust in Him?
• Where does the image of God as a bird appear?
• How do you imagine God?
• How do you feel about imagining God as a bird or any other image?
• What are some of your mental pictures of God?
• When might reading this particular psalm be comforting to you or someone else?
• In Luke 13 what are the circumstances in which Jesus says these things about Jerusalem?
• What are the events that Jesus alludes to in the first 3 verses?
• Why can Jesus not gather Jerusalem close to himself?
• How do you think Jesus felt at this time?

Retracing Your Steps
Attach the birds and the words of the key verse on a clothesline. Have the children arrange the birds and cards in the correct order.

Using the worksheet "God Is Like," help the children discover other images that give us a better understanding of God's love. (Answers: burning bush, holy, pure; patient and forgiving father; generous employer; searching thankful shepherd; relentless woman searching for a coin, thankful; light, salvation, comfort; rock, refuge, protection; king of all the earth, mighty, strong; builder, caring; maker of garments, caring; mother, comforting)

Stepping Beyond

Help newcomers assemble their Advent wreaths. Review for them the purpose and use of the wreaths. Encourage the children to decorate their third candle with the image of the bird. Provide soft, colored molding wax to attach to the candles, or allow the children to make candle cups in the shapes of birds. They may also make additional origami cranes and place these on both sides of the candle.

Encourage discussion about the images we have of God, even some we may have outgrown (ex: Santa Claus). Remind the children of the present image of God that we have in Jesus. Ask them to share what Jesus revealed about God's love for us.

Stepping Out

Gather the children together for closure. Ask them to share their favorite images of God from today's study. Pray that each child will continue to look forward to Jesus' coming and to grow in their knowledge and understanding of who God is and how God appears.

God Is Like . . .

Jesus describes his love for Jerusalem as that of a mother hen wanting to gather her chicks safely in. What other images help us to better understand God's love? Write the image described in each Scripture passage.

Genesis 3:3-6   _____

Luke 15:11-32   _____

Matthew 20:1-15   _____

Luke 15:4-7   _____

Luke 15:8-10   _____

Psalm 27:1   _____

2 Samuel 22:2   _____

Psalm 47:7   _____

Hebrews 3:4   _____

Genesis 3:21   _____

Isaiah 66:13   _____

The Fourth Sunday of Advent
Love the Star Is on the Way

John 1:1-14

PREPARING FOR THE JOURNEY

The metaphors given in John 1 for Christ, Word, and Light are familiar. In Genesis the same phrase, "in the beginning," connotes something that occurred at the beginning of time, whereas here it tells of One who was there in the beginning, before time and the world. We expect to read, "In the beginning, . . . God."

John wrote to an audience he assumed was familiar with the idea of "The Word," obviously for his own disciples who would know his teachings and common phrases. It is the preeminent metaphor for God, which perhaps is "enlightened" by our key verse about the "true Light." Although John said the Word was God, he did not say God was the Word. In his commentary on John, George Beasley-Murray describes this light or "star" thus:

> The light of the Logos shone in the primal darkness at creation, . . . amid the darkness of fallen mankind; . . . with greater brilliance in the glory of the Incarnate One; and it shines on in the era of the Resurrection, which is the time of the Paraclete."

It is for such a star that we look to come, which came, is present, and is coming again. It is also that to which we, like John, are to be "stars" (witnesses) that lead others to the Light.

Key Verse
The true Light, which enlightens everyone, was coming into the world. John 1:9

Key Concept
The purpose of Jesus' coming is always to bring light to darkness, to enlighten us to God's ways and will.

Educational Aims

To continue to build upon the spiritual anticipation of Christmas, to learn about the navigational value of stars, to explore ways of being "stars" that lead others to Christ

Resources You Will Need

<u>Stepping In</u>
biblical costumes, a large star hanging over a makeshift manger, someone to provide information about traveling or navigating according to the stars, a map with constellations

<u>Stepping Up</u>
taped recording of "People, Look East" and printed words of stanza 4 and the refrain, a Bible for each child, pantomime plan for Bible reading

<u>Retracing Your Steps</u>
Bibles, concordances, paper, pencils

<u>Stepping Beyond</u>
supplies for individual Advents wreaths: greenery, circular styrofoam forms, candles and soft colored molding wax, scissors, glue gun, glue sticks

<u>Stepping Out</u>
fourth Advent candle and a white Christ candle to take home

<u>Before You Teach</u>
Familiarize yourself with John 1:1-14. Make plans for the children to present it in mime with a narrator.

GUIDING THE JOURNEY

Stepping In

Display in a prominent place a life-size manger containing some hay and a large star hanging over it. As the children arrive, direct them to choose costumes to act out the day's Bible reading. Assign parts for a narrator; God (white costume); Jesus (white costume with red sash); John (brown costume, suggestive of camel hair); and different individuals or groups who will receive the light, know the light, and reject the light.

After everyone is dressed in costume, let the visitor talk about navigating by the stars. Point out on a map of constellations the North Star, the Big and Little Dippers, Orion, and other well-known images.

Explain: Today we are focusing on Love the Star Is on the Way. During this session we will consider how we can be "stars" that lead people to God.

Stepping Up

Play the recording of "People, Look East." Distribute song sheets of stanza 4 and the refrain. Sing the song together. Assign a child to light the fourth candle of the class Advent wreath.

Have the children turn in their Bibles to John 1:1-14. Suggest ways to pantomime the story, or allow the children to make suggestions. Ask the narrator to read it slowly. Explain how this is a worshipful response to the story, not a performance of it.

Suggested Movements
- (v. 1) God stands with outstretched hands. Jesus is immediately behind, making the same motions.
- (v. 2) God and Jesus intertwine their arms.
- (v. 3) Jesus steps forward and puts on a red sash. He rolls his arms and stops with palms facing outward.
- (v. 4) Two or three people kneel before him, looking dejected with bowed heads. Jesus touches his right hand to his lips and blows toward them. They rise.
- (v. 5) God gives Jesus a light (large candle), which Jesus holds up.
- (v. 6) John kneels before God and then rises with a light (small candle).

- (vv. 7-8) John moves toward the people with his light. They circle him.
- (vv. 9-10) Jesus moves toward the people with his light. They look at Jesus, and then away.
- (v. 11) Another group looks at Jesus and turns, holding their hands in front of their faces.
- (v. 12) The last group comes to Jesus, kneels, holds up a small candle.
- (v. 13) God takes Jesus' candle and lights each one.
- (v. 14) God steps back with hands held out. Jesus returns to his position behind God.

Storyteller's Questions
- How did the story "feel" to you?
- What does this passage tell us about the relationship of God to the Word?
- Do you think some who accepted John rejected Jesus? Why or why not?
- Why do people not know Jesus?
- What does it mean to be a child of God?
- How are we born of God?
- What does Jesus show us about God?

Retracing Your Steps
Using Bibles and concordances, have the children look up other Scripture passages about light and darkness. Make 2 groups to compare and contrast the effects of light and darkness in our lives. Let individuals choose a verse they particularly like to be read in closing time.

Stepping Beyond
Help newcomers or absentees make their candles or wreaths. Have all supplies available. The children will decorate their fourth candle, the star candle. Encourage them to share ways they see themselves as "stars," and how or why being a "light" for Christ is difficult. Ask them to share ways they see Christ's light in the world, the church, their family, and themselves.

Stepping Out

Gather the children together for closure. Give each child a candle. Light your candle from the large candle "Jesus" was holding, and then let each child read the verse they chose earlier as they light their candle. Close by thanking God for the light of Christ that darkness can never overcome and by asking God for help in being lights for Christ.

Youth

The First Sunday of Advent
Love the Guest Is on the Way

Matthew 25:31-46

Youth Learning Tension
• How does the "strangeness" of Jesus change the way we prepare for him coming as a guest?

Stanza 1 of "People, Look East" suggests we prepare our homes for the coming of a guest. "Make your house fair as you are able. Trim the hearth and set the table." If Christ came to your house, would he be welcome? Would you feel comfortable with him, or would you perceive him to be alien and strange? John 1:10-11 gives us a clue. "He was in the world, and the world came into being through him. He came to what was his own, and his own people did not accept him." Christ came into this world as a stranger, born in a stable.

Welcoming Christ as a guest in our house or church is like welcoming a stranger. Strangers or guests might be spoken of in three ways. One group may be outsiders who dress, speak, and act differently than we do. They may be of a different class, culture, race, or age. Others may not be obvious outsiders. They fit somewhere between the obvious outsiders and the intimate insiders. But they may be passive observers rather than intimate participants. There are also the differences that exist in any relationship between two persons. This is most obvious with outsiders, less obvious with inside strangers or guests, and even less noticeable with those of regular contact. Even with our closest friends and family members there remain significant differences. This "strangeness" remains even in our ability to know ourselves. At what times do we feel most strange with ourselves?

About Matthew 25:31-46

Our Scripture passage talks about the coming of Jesus as King and God. All the angels are his friends and cohorts. All the nations are gathered before his judgment throne. Those before the throne know Jesus, but he may seem strange and different because he identifies with the poor and oppressed. What happens when Jesus comes? Notice that nothing is said about grace, confession, faith, or forgiveness of sins. What counts is whether or not one has acted with loving care for the "different" ones. Jesus calls them "the least of these who are my brothers and sisters."

What is the main point of the scene? When people respond or fail to respond to human need, they are responding or failing to respond to Christ. This turns out to be a rude awakening, a surprise. The people ask, "When did we see you like this?" Each person is singled out and asked this question. "I was a stranger. Did you invite me in?" They are surprised by the question. "When did we see you as a stranger?" they ask. Jesus singles each one out and asks, "What have you done with people who are different and strange—the hungry, the thirsty, the homeless, the naked, the physically afflicted, and the prisoner? When you have done it to them, you have done it to me."

Our Story

Invite each youth to complete the worksheet "What Do You Prefer?" (p. 97). Ask the following questions:

• Which column of actions seems to be closest to your preferences?
• Which actions seem to be most strange or alien?
• What are some other characteristics of strangers?
• How would any of these actions relate to seeing Jesus as strange?

The inventory suggests other characteristics that can cause us to see others as strangers [ex: relationships, ways of communicating, use of space and time, ways of learning]. Would Jesus seem like a stranger to us in any of these ways?

The Larger Story

Read the story of guests and strangers coming to the tent of Abraham and Sarah (Gen 18:1-21). When the three strangers approached them from the desert, Abraham and Sarah did not know who they were. At first these strangers were small spots on the horizon. As they approached, they took on human shape and finally had faces. Abraham and Sarah did not know who they were hosting. They were simply carrying out the command of God to be hospitable to the stranger or alien as revealed in Leviticus 19:33-34.

> When an alien [stranger] resides with you in your land, you shall not oppress the alien. The alien who resides with you shall be as a citizen among you; you shall love the alien as yourself, for you were aliens in the land of Egypt: I am the Lord your God.

Why do strangers among us need to be loved and protected? Did Jesus need to be protected at his birth? [Yes. Herod threatened to kill him.] What are some examples of hospitality toward Jesus at his birth? [the opening of the stable when there was no room in the inn, the gifts of the wise men]

As an adult, Jesus enters the scene as one who is a guest in need of hospitality. But the roles of guest and host are soon reversed. At the marriage feast in Cana, Jesus comes as a guest, but soon is changing water to wine and providing the necessary means for the wedding feast to continue. At the home of Simon the Pharisee, Jesus comes as the guest, although he responds to the act of the woman anointing his feet by telling a story and proclaiming God's forgiveness. On the road to Emmaus on Easter Sunday evening, a stranger joins two of Jesus' disciples. When they reach the home of the disciples, Jesus is the one who takes bread and blesses it and reveals himself as the Lord. In the act of sharing bread with a stranger, they recognize the risen Lord.

What could we do in preparation for the coming of Christ that would awaken us to the strangeness of the season? We have been there so many times that everything seems commonplace. Brainstorm some ways that both church and home could deepen the awareness of Jesus' coming as a stranger.

Intersection

Display on a simple table the communion elements of bread and cup. Ask: Who is the guest, and who is the host at this table? Do we invite Jesus to this table, or does Jesus invite us? This is not our table; this is the Lord's table. And it is called the Lord's Supper. Jesus is the host at this supper. Jesus is the one who issues the invitation and desires our presence. Jesus says to us, "Be my guest," and we respond by gathering around the table. What kind of responses do we make when we are invited as a guest to someone's table?

Does communion at Christmas seem to be a contradiction? In the midst of celebrating the birth of Jesus we pause to commemorate his death. Someone has said that the shadow of the cross falls across the manger. Think of ways that birth and death are closely tied. But to think of Jesus' death at the time of his birth seems to strike a discordant note. Read the closing sentences of Dee Brown's *Bury My Heart at Wounded Knee*. After the massacre of the Sioux at Wounded Knee, South Dakota, in 1890, the wounded survivors were hauled to the post in wagons.

> The wagon loads of wounded Sioux (4 men and 47 women and children) reached Pine Ridge after dark. Because all available barracks were filled with soldiers, they were left lying in the open wagons in the bitter cold while an inept army officer searched for shelter. Finally the Episcopal mission was opened, the benches taken out, and hay scattered over the rough flooring.
>
> It was the fourth day after Christmas in the year of our Lord 1890. When the first torn and bleeding bodies were carried into the candlelit church, those who were conscious could see Christmas greenery hanging from the open rafters. Across the chancel front above the pulpit was strung a crudely lettered banner: PEACE ON EARTH, GOOD WILL TO MEN.

This all seems so contradictory. But when we think about it, Christmas is a perfect time to celebrate communion. We not only remember Christ's death; we also celebrate his continuing presence in our midst. Christ is born. Christ has died. Christ has risen. Christ shall come again. Christmas is a time of contradictions: remembering death at the time of birth, strangers becoming friends, guests becoming hosts.

Calling

Read Hebrews 13:1-2. The writer of Hebrews calls on us to show hospitality to strangers. Hospitality is easy when you know someone. Our doors open to our friends, and they come and go as they please. But hospitality goes a step further by welcoming the stranger. Consider some of the following possibilities:

• Hospice centers are planned for the terminally ill who receive care they need. Attendants are trained to minister with compassion to patients as they face death.

• Hospitality becomes very focused for people who have cancer or AIDS. The dread of these diseases is realistically faced and medically met.

• People who have felt at home all of their lives suddenly become "strangers" in old age. Aging people want to retain their dignity as they enter the twilight years. Retirement homes and nursing homes are options when people can no longer live independently.

• The courts are filled with cases involving abused children. Less visible are cases of abused parents. Abused people are left with the feeling of being "strangers on the earth."

• Cities are filled with street people, those who find no permanent home or shelter and no food promised. Homeless people need protection and hope for the sustenance that keeps them alive.

• Prison reform is expected in many sections of the country. Prisons are crowded and will not meet existing demands. There is much indecision about rehabilitation and which crimes deserve the severest punishment.

Are these the contemporary "strangers" Jesus talked about in Matthew 25? When we minister to the "least of these," are we ministering to Jesus?

What Do You Prefer?

Identify your preferences along the continuum by circling one of the dots.

Using words to communicate	• • • • •	Using gestures to communicate
Being rational and logical	• • • • •	Being emotional and spontaneous
Being by myself	• • • • •	Being with a group
Having a large, less close circle of friends	• • • • •	Having a small, close circle of friends
Describing myself based on my accomplishments	• • • • •	Describing myself based on my relationships
Doing one thing at a time	• • • • •	Doing a variety of things at once
Keeping a time schedule	• • • • •	Going with the flow
Consulting many sources	• • • • •	Going with the best authority
Figuring things out for myself	• • • • •	Following someone else's example
Avoiding conflict	• • • • •	Dealing directly with conflict
Having private space	• • • • •	Sharing space
Being quick and learning something efficiently	• • • • •	Being accurate and learning something well

The Second Sunday of Advent
Love the Rose Is on the Way

2 Corinthians 2:14-17

Youth Learning Tension
• How does the sense of smell evoke the memory of Christ and awake faith?

Nothing triggers memory more than a smell. One scent can explode softly in our memory like a land mine bringing back memories long forgotten. Sherlock Holmes, the master detective, said there are 75 different smells a criminal expert should be able to distinguish. Most people think they could not possibly do such a thing, but experiences with smell tell us differently.

Someone has said that smell is the mute sense, the one without words. The link between smells and the language centers of our brains are pitifully weak. Although our sense of smell gives us direct contact with the outside world, smells are difficult to describe as noted from experiments we do with our eyes closed. Not so with the connections between smells and memory.

The tiniest of scents can awaken our memories in moments. Smells help us remember, and "remember" is a big word when it comes to our faith. Perhaps that is what the apostle Paul means when he says that "Christ always leads us in triumphal procession, and through us spreads in every place the fragrance that comes from knowing him. For we are the aroma of Christ" (2 Cor 2:14-15). Perhaps our hymn has this in mind as we sing, "Love the Rose is on the way."

About 2 Corinthians 2:14-17
When Paul breaks into a thought pattern with "thanks be to God," he is usually remembering something that makes him thankful. He remembers a triumphal procession where a famous general is coming home to a huge celebration after years of absence. Around the victor's path are clouds of incense that spread a fragrance in every direction.

This is the way the knowledge of God is spread, imparting freedom, life, confidence, joy, and hope. Paul reminds us that we are the aroma of

Christ. The aroma that came from Christ was an aroma of sacrifice. This sacrifice is a fragrance well pleasing to God. "Christ loved us and gave himself up for us, a fragrant offering and sacrifice to God" (Eph 5:2). But people respond to the fragrance of Christ in different ways.

To those who are perishing, it is a fragrance of death. In smelling it they are reminded of death. They are repelled and disgusted by it. But to those being saved, it is the fragrance of life. It is like the aroma from the garden on resurrection morning! In other words, the aroma of Christ has different effects on people, much like the sense of smell touches us and evokes memories in us in many different ways.

Our Story
Distribute pencils and paper. Ask youth to record the first memory that comes to their mind when they hear each of the following phrases. Describe the memory with a word or a short sentence.

• the smell of life
• the smell of death
• the smell of victory
• the smell of defeat
• the smell of love
• the smell of hope
• the smell of sickness
• the smell of health

Explain how difficult it may seem to put words to smells. Smells usually evoke memories more than descriptions of smells. Ask group members to share memories of strong scents and the memories these scents bring to mind. Recall Carl Sandburg's description of Jesus:

This Jesus was good to look at, smelled good, listened good. Something fresh and beautiful came from the skin of his body and the touch of his hands wherever he passed along.

How could Sandburg make a statement such as this? [good memories of freshness and beauty, a vivid imagination about Jesus]

The Larger Story

Lead a Bible study about the ways perfumes and fragrances are used in the Bible. Assign various texts to be read, and then comment on each text.

Balm is an aromatic resin used for cosmetic and medical purposes. Genesis 43:11 refers to balm as a yellow aromatic resin. Balm was exported from Gilead to Egypt and Phoenicia to be used for healing purposes (Gen 37:25; Ezek 27:17). When we sing the old song, "There is a balm in Gilead that heals a sin-sick soul," we are not only singing about its healing properties, but also the suggestive aroma that brings healing. Jeremiah said, "Is there no balm in Gilead? Is there no physician there? Why then has the health of my poor people not been restored" (Jer 8:22)?

God seemed to be sniffing aromas more than people. When Noah offered burnt animal sacrifices at the ebbing of the flood, "the Lord smelled the pleasing odor [and] said in his heart, 'I will never again curse the ground because of humankind'" (Gen 8:21). A clear sign of God's rejection of our worship is in God's refusal to smell the offering we bring (Lev 26:31; Amos 5:21). God dwells in unseen, thick darkness within the Holy of Holies, yet God's presence is made real in the "whiffing" of the smells offered to Him (1 Kgs 8:12; 2 Chron 2:4).

The importance of the power of smell in scripture can be summed up in Job 14:9. Even if a tree is cut down and the roots grow old in the earth and its stump dies in the ground, "Yet at the scent of water it will bud and put forth branches like a young plant." Smell is considered to be a life-giving force.

In the New Testament the most prized gifts were gifts of sweet aromas. The gifts the Magi brought to Jesus were perfumes—frankincense and myrrh (Matt 2:11). Frankincense was an ingredient used in perfume for the most holy place in the tabernacle (Exod 30:23). Myrrh was used as an ingredient in anointing oil (Exod 30:23) and applied as a perfume (Esther 2:12). Aloe is a large tree that produces resin and oil used in making perfume. Nicodemus anointed the body of Jesus with a mixture of aloe and myrrh. Nard was an expensive fragrance coming from the roots of an herb. It was used by the woman anointing Jesus at Simon's house in Bethany (Mark 14:3; John 12:3). Because of the expense of the perfume, the woman was rebuked for the "waste" when the sale of the perfume could have been used for more practical purposes.

Intersection
Write the following statements on slips of paper or note cards. Distribute the papers to youth. Read each statement. Ask: What insight does the statement give about the birth, life, death, and resurrection of Jesus?

- Just remember in the winter far beneath the bitter snows, lies the seed that with the sun's love in the spring becomes the rose.
- A rose, pleasing to the eye and to the nose . . .
- Smells are surer than sights and sounds to warm the heartstrings.
- Always remember, a rose will grow anywhere.
- When we give perfume to someone, we give them liquid memory.
- Roses work their way through the hard ground of defeat more easily than through success.
- Lo, how a rose e'er blooming from tender stem hath sprung.
- Roses drench our senses with exquisite smells.
- I am a rose of Sharon, a lily of the valleys (Song of Sol 2:1).
- The wilderness and the dry land shall be glad, the desert shall rejoice and blossom (Isa 35:1).

Recall how fragrances are used in the Bible—healing, sacrifice, anointing, beauty, etc. What do these purposes say about the birth, life, death, and resurrection of Jesus?

Calling
Place a rose on a small table in the center of the group. If possible, put a spotlight on the rose and leave the rest of the room in darkness. Spend five minutes in silence, simply gazing on the rose and picking up the scent of the rose in the room. Following the period of silence, ask group members to share memories that came to mind.

Recall the story of the anointing of Jesus at Bethany (John 12:1-8). The house is said to have been filled with the fragrance of the ointment. What is the meaning of John's statement? The fragrance of the ointment filled the house in the same way that the fragrance of the gospel will fill the church and eventually the whole world. Close with this phrase: "But thanks be to God, who in Christ always leads us in triumph and through us spreads the fragrance of him everywhere."

The Third Sunday of Advent
Love the Bird Is on the Way

Luke 13:31-34

Youth Learning Tension
- How is the gathering activity of birds an important image for the gathering of God's people?
- What does the Bible say about Jesus as one who gathers?

To our forefathers and mothers, birds were the manifestation of gods and spirits, the messengers of heavenly beings that announced new situations in advance and served as guides to human decision making. The dove announced the appearance of dry land to Noah and proclaimed the blessing of God on Jesus at his baptism in the Jordan River.

One way of discovering what God is doing is to watch the birds. The fancy word is ornithology, a study of zoology dealing with birds and bird watching. Although God loves birds and cares for them, birds remain eternally busy. Birds live around us and over us, moving rapidly in a 3-dimensional world and always seeming to know where they are going.

Do you want to become a bird watcher? Then you will need to escape the busy city streets, the shopping centers, and the major freeways. Find your way to the remote, out-of-the-way places of ponds, wetlands, marshes, and swamps. Become comfortable with quiet natural settings. Learn to look carefully at the insignificant and the small. Learn from the birds the meaning of time and place. "Even the stork in the heavens knows its times; and the turtledove, swallow, and crane observe the time of their coming; but my people do not know the ordinance of the Lord" (Jer 8:7). Perhaps then you will know that Jesus is on the way because "Love the Bird is on the way."

About Luke 13:31-34
Jesus declares that he will not be stopped by Herod from going to Jerusalem. There he will be killed, like all prophets who die in Jerusalem. Two animals give us the picture of the alternatives. Some animals are very dangerous. Here Herod is pictured as a devouring fox. In Genesis 3, Satan is

described as a serpent. According to 1 Peter 5:8, the devil roams around like a lion looking for prey. John 10:12 speaks of how the wolf grabs the sheep from the protection of the sheepfold.

In contrast, the protecting and nurturing God is pictured as a bird, in this situation a mothering hen that draws her young under her wings when danger threatens their safety. We live in a farming household of threatening and protecting forces. The world is a very dangerous place. Evil theatens to devour us in the form of Herod the fox. The mother bird is anxious because her young are exposed and will not accept protection. She must stand up to the cruel fox and protect her young. But what happens to the young when they will not find shelter and protection under the mother bird's wings?

Have you ever loved someone you could not protect? Do you understand why it is so difficult for parents to let you go? You may understand the depth of anguish in Jesus' words. All the mother bird can do is open her wings. And there she is in a most vulnerable posture—wings spread and breast exposed. There she stands between all of us and those who would do us harm. She has nothing to protect with except her willingness and her body. If the fox wants her children, he will have to kill her first. Which is exactly what Herod does to Jesus. And all those under his wings scatter. What will it take to bring them back together?

Our Story

Gather materials for building nests (sticks, grass, leaves, moss, mud, string, scraps, feathers). Divide the group into smaller groups of 3 or 4. Allow 15 minutes for groups to create a nest, using their imagination and creativity. Following this creative effort, ask these questions:

• Imagine being a bird that is in the process of building a nest. What difficulties would you have? [weather, finding materials, other birds stealing your supplies]

• What must a bird do to build a nest? [keep busy, overcome difficulties]

- Is building a nest a solitary activity or one that takes a joint effort? [In many cases mother, father, and other birds that are "helpers of the nest" join in the activity.]

- What is the purpose of nests and nesting? [giving birth, warmth, safety, feeding, preparation for flying]

- Can nests be built almost anywhere? [Yes. Birds are found everywhere in the world. No habitat seems to be closed to them. Nests are found on the ground, floating in water, and in bushes and trees and on cliffs. They can be slight scrapes on the ground or large elaborate structures.]

- Can you think of ways that a nest is like your home or church?

- Why would Jesus say he was like a mother bird gathering her brood under her wings (Luke 13:34)?

The Larger Story

Birds are often pictured in scripture as describing the activity of God. Assign the following passages to group members. Ask that the text be read. Lead a discussion. Describe the activity of God.

- Exodus 19:4—Moses reminds the people that God saved them by bearing them up "on eagle's wings" and bringing them to himself.

- Exodus 16:3—Flocks of quail providentially provided Israel with food in the wilderness wanderings (see Ps 105:40).

- Isaiah 40:31—The people will "mount up with wings like eagles," the exhilaration of release and freedom and the promise of sustenance through the long pilgrim journey home from exile.

- Psalm 57:1—In the shadow of God's wings the people will take refuge until the storms of life pass.

- Psalm 84:3—This is a picture of our true well-being when we find sanctuary in God's house.

- Deuteronomy 32:11—Like an eagle the Lord stirs up the nest and hovers over the young.

- Jeremiah 8:7—God's people lose their way, but the birds have an "internal compass." They know their way.

- Matthew 3:16—The Spirit of God rests on Jesus just as the spirit of God "broods" over the waters (see Gen 1:2).

- Matthew 6:26—Do not be anxious about the necessities of life. Be as free from care as the birds. God cares for them.

- Matthew 10:29—God protects and cares for us. Not one sparrow falls to the ground without God's purposes.

Intersection

If we watch the birds, we will discover that they are always gathering—into nests, under wings, and into flocks. Jesus said, "I have been like a mother bird trying to gather you." In gathering, God's people become a people. In gathering, we are called a church, an assembly, and a community. The act of gathering is the primary act of Christian people.

The word for "gathering" is the same word used in the New Testament for "synagogue," meaning to assemble or bring together. Remember that the important words in the Bible are relational words—fathers, mothers, sons, daughters, brothers, sisters, and disciples. Meetings of Christians were gatherings of people in relationship with one another—a gathering of "family." Simply being together is an act of grace, an action parable of God's presence among us. Before Christians do anything else, they gather, and in the gathering proclaim belief in the resurrected Christ. The early Christians were martyred simply for meeting together. The promises of gathering and the dangers of scattering are strong themes in the Bible and remind us that "Love the Bird" is one who gathers rather than scatters.

Assign the following passages to group members. Describe the results of gathering and scattering.

Gathering
- Psalms 106:47—The Psalmist cries that the Lord will save the people by gathering them.

- Numbers 11:4—A number of strangers are gathered into a people.

- Isaiah 40:11—God feeds the flock and gathers them into His arms.

- Matthew 18:20—Jesus promises to be present wherever 2 or 3 are gathered in his name.

- 1 Corinthians 14:26—The earliest Christians understood themselves as coming together, gathered, and brought into a shared life, living together in the presence and praise of God.

- John 11:52—Jesus is born, lives, and dies, not for the nations only, but to gather into one the children of God who are scattered abroad.

- Ephesians 1:10—God's plan, which will be completed when the time is right, is to bring all creation together.

Scattering
- Deuteronomy 4:27—Scattering is seen as the punishment of God. The Lord scatters the people and leaves them few in number.

- Matthew 12:30—Gathering is the task of Christian discipleship. "Whoever does not gather with me scatters."

- Luke 1:51—Mary has confidence in God's ability to turn the tables on the lofty and proud and to "scatter" them.

- Matthew 25:24, 26—Through the ideas of sowing and reaping, Matthew contrasts scattering and gathering.

• Acts 5:36—Gamaliel tells the story of Theudas who gathered 400 followers, but was killed. "All who followed him were dispersed and disappeared."

Calling

Someone has said that it is the task of the family to give children "roots and wings." Families that have let children go are said to have "empty nests." Why are children "called" to leave home?

The task of families is to bless those who leave home with the hope that the person leaving will be able to go it alone successfully. "Go fly" is the blessing parents give to their children. When parents say "go fly," they are saying several things.

A blessing reaffirms ties that will naturally remain. A blessing binds us to a past and gives us permission to return. A blessing confirms our membership in a family, a "nest," and does not sever us from it. A blessing lets us go with grace. The mother bird that gives us the warmth and protection of the nest also provides us with the skill and the courage to leave the nest and "fly."

Stanza 3 of "People, Look East" speaks of fledging time.

> Birds, though you long have ceased to build,
> Guard the nest that must be filled.
> Even the hour when wings are frozen
> God for fledging time has chosen.

Fledging time is God's time, the right moment for flying. The task of parents is to make us ready for "flight" and independent action. Ask the following questions:

• Did God have the "right time" in mind for Jesus? [Yes. Read Gal 4:4.]

• What experiences have you had that prepare you for flight? [spending time away from home, camp and retreat experiences]

• What is the difference between leaving home and scattering? [Scattering leaves us isolated and alone. When we leave home with blessing, we can always come back.]

The Fourth Sunday of Advent
Love the Star Is on the Way

Revelation 22:16

Youth Learning Tension
• How do youth return to an experience of mystery, awe, and reverence during the Advent season?

Early in May 1998, astrologists watched in utter amazement the birth of planets, as sky watchers spied a planetary construction zone in exactly the same process that apparently formed earth and the other planets of our solar system 4.5 billion years ago. Here was a startling and stunning discovery, the creation of planets caught in the act. Scientists concluded that if a star is not too old and not too young, not too big and not too small, not too hot and not too cold, then it is practically inevitable that planets will form around such a star. Planets are the first prerequisites for life, and when a star is born, life is possible.

Modern technology helps us see farther. The creation of seeing devices such as the Hubble space telescope, launched into space in the early 1990s, lifts us beyond the haze of earth's environment into the far reaches of outer space. These discoveries can give us new understandings of our existence and return to us the awe and mystery our souls so desperately need. We will be amazed, much like the early disciples "gazing up toward heaven," and we will find new meanings in "Love the Star is on the way."

About Revelation 22:16
A testimony is a declaration of who one is and what one claims for oneself. Jesus testifies to all the churches then and now. He says, "I am the root and the descendent of David, the bright morning star." In Revelation 5:5 the Lamb is described as "the Lion of the tribe of Judah, the Root of David." John now focuses on the transcendent and glorified Christ. Paul's testimony is similar. "He is the image of the invisible God, the firstborn of all creation" (Col 1:15).

How should we identify Jesus as the morning star? Possibly this can be related to the words of Numbers 24:17, "a star shall come out of Jacob." The final promise to the church at Thyratira was that Christ would give to the conquering martyrs "the morning star" (Rev 2:28), a symbol of a new life and a new day. Jesus identifies himself as this bright and morning star whom all people of faith will see in God's new age. This is the same image described in 2 Peter 1:19, "You will do well to be attentive to this as to a lamp shining in a dark place, until the day dawns and the morning star rises in your hearts." Like the morning star, Peter announces the shining brightness of a day that is coming. "Until the day dawns" refers to the second coming of Christ, which ends the world's darkness as the rising sun ends the darkness of the night.

Two different words are used for star in Revelation 2:28 and 2 Peter 1:19. Revelation 2:28 may be alluding to Venus, referring not only to beauty, but to brightness. This is the star that shines brightest in the early morning when the skies are darkest and continues to shine long after the sun is up. The morning star in 2 Peter 1:19 may mean the sun, the source of light, which springs up to dispel the darkness of the night. Both proclaim the good news that Christ is the light coming into the world (John 1:9). Our hymn, "People, Look East," says it clearly and correctly: "Shining beyond the frosty weather, bright as the sun and moon together."

Our Story
Ask group members to share experiences of transcendence. Explain that transcendence extends or lies beyond the limits of ordinary experience and brings us to a sense of awe and mystery. Ask what youth mean when they say something is "awesome." Explain that awe may carry with it dread, fear, mystery, and reverence. Recall the words of the hymn "How Great Thou Art": "O Lord my God! When I in awesome wonder consider all the worlds Thy hands have made." Listed below are some ways group members may experience moments of transcendence.

• Times of day—night, day, morning, evening, dawn, sunrise, sunset
• Common life—sleeping, dreaming, praying, eating, working, studying, playing

- Vastness of the universe—sun, moon, stars, watches of the night, the whole created order, the heavens and the earth
- Mysteries of life and death—young, old, illnesses, accidents, healings, births

Group members may choose any of these moments or others that evoke a sense of mystery and awe.

The Larger Story
Divide the larger group into triads (groups of 3). Give each group the following Scripture passages, but without the explanatory notes. Ask each group to describe the ways stars are referenced in the Bible, and then to report on one of the references.

- Genesis 1:16—The stars, like the sun and moon, are the creation of God.

- Genesis 22:17—The most frequent use of stars is in reference to their incalculable number. Abraham will be blessed and given offspring "as numerous as the stars in heaven."

- Numbers 24:17—A leader is referred to as a "star," possibly a reference to the coming Messiah.

- Deuteronomy 1:10—The blessings of God are as numerous as the stars in heaven.

- Deuteronomy 4:19—The people are warned not to follow astrology and the worship of stars.

- Job 3:9—Darkened stars are associated with suffering and judgment when they fail to give their light.

- Isaiah 34:4—The end of time is described by turbulent changes in the sky. "All the host of heaven shall rot away, and the skies roll up like a scroll."

• Daniel 12:3—Wise and righteous people are described as stars.

• Matthew 24:29—Jesus speaks of the suffering at the end of time when the stars will fall from heaven.

• Acts 27:20—Stars were needed as guides for navigation at sea.

• Revelation 1:16, 20—Seven stars are held in the right hand of the one who discloses himself to John. The stars are "the angels of the seven churches."

Following these readings and discussion, brainstorm the way these images might be descriptive of Jesus as "the bright and morning star" [blessing, beauty, wisdom, a leader and a guide, bringing judgment, a messenger from God].

Intersection
Read Matthew 2:1-10. Explain that the star is mentioned in verses 2, 7, 9, and 10, but nowhere else in the New Testament. Ask, "What is distinctive about the star of Bethlehem?" Lead a discussion including some of the following points.

• The question concerning the purpose of the star is answered in verse 2: "We observed his star at its rising, and have come to pay him homage."

• The star publicizes the birth of Jesus and draws the wise men toward him.

• The star remains stationary while the wise men are in Jerusalem. It then leads them not only to Bethlehem but to the precise location where it "stopped" to mark the spot where Jesus was born (v. 9).

• They do not admire or study the star, but follow it, even to the point of resisting the political powers.

• The star may be a fulfillment of Old Testament prophecies (Num 24:14-17). God can use the mistaken ideas of astrology to lead people to the knowledge of Christ.

Calling

For biblical people, the sky was filled with amazement, awe, and wonder. Luke records that the disciples were "gazing up toward heaven" (Acts 1:10). In this final scene of the earthly story of Jesus, their eyes were fixed on the sky. According to Luke, Jesus was "lifted up, and a cloud took him out of their sight" (v. 9).

Ask group members to picture this scene in their minds and describe how it happened. Following their responses, explain that the church never seemed to be too concerned about how this happened. This event is a matter of faith, and faith always leads us to mystery. When Jesus' followers have lifted their eyes toward the sky and have caught a vision of Jesus as the ascended Lord, they are able to see farther and more clearly than they have ever seen before. When people are looking "up" into the heavens, they are looking beyond all earthly situations into the realm where God's purposes are accomplished and where all love, power, goodness, and justice are bound together in wholeness. The Bible speaks of Jesus descending to become one with us and ascending to again become one with God.

Read Colossians 1:15-20. Explain that the book of Colossians was written to Christians who were trying to follow Christ in the midst of an evil and pagan world. They had to keep their eyes lifted up toward a morning star that introduced the dawn of a new day. The new day gives us a new way of understanding our lives.

Adults

The First Sunday of Advent
Love the Guest Is on the Way

Isaiah 40:3-11

Core Highlights
• Christian Life
• Theology and Doctrine

Central Questions
• How can we prepare to celebrate the coming of Christ?
• How can our preparation time also be worship time?

Focusing Our Vision
The title of our lesson comes from a 20th-century English carol entitled "People, Look East." Each of the first 4 stanzas of this Advent hymn imagines Christ in the form of a different object. Love is a guest, a rose, a bird, and a star. Finally the Lord comes to set "every peak and valley humming." This phrase from the last stanza of the hymn captures the spirit of the Scripture text well.

The prophet Isaiah announces the promise of a coming triumph. After the warfare has ended and the sins have been pardoned, God will arrive. "Make straight in the desert a highway for our God. Every valley shall be lifted up, and every mountain and hill will be made low" (vv. 3-4). The cataclysm that the voice from the wilderness calls for is nothing less than the overthrow of the old routine, the old maps, a complete remaking of our spiritual geography. Be prepared! Love is on the way.

Advent is the season of preparation. In the traditional church calendar it marks the beginning of the Christian year. The four weeks before Christmas are set aside to rehearse the prophecies of the Hebrew scriptures and the stories leading up to the Bethlehem birth. Many Christians through the ages have found that Advent is a wonderful counterpoint to the way the rest of the world celebrates the weeks preceding Christmas.

113

Instead of rushing into Christmas carols before Thanksgiving, the Advent season invites us into a time of anticipation and preparation.

The four lessons in this series each build on one of the images found in the English hymn. We will encounter some new and ancient pictures of the promised Christ. We will use those pictures to reimagine our own positions in relationship to God. We will turn our attention toward the worship of God during this time of preparation.

That preparation, however, in the vision of Isaiah is not a routine housecleaning or schedule adjustment. Instead, the prophet imagines a radical overhaul. Everything must be brought into line; the proclamation must go out; the people must be prepared.

Listening to the Story
The passage that forms the text for this lesson actually opens the last half of the book of Isaiah. The first 39 chapters deal with the sins of the people and the punishment God will bring against them as discipline. Chapter 40, however, changes the tone drastically with its opening phrases, "Comfort, O comfort my people." Comfort, restoration, redemption, and victory become the themes of the latter part of this prophetic book. These were the words addressed to the Jewish people in the Babylonian captivity. They come as a promise that the exiles have not been abandoned or forgotten. Love is on the way.

Franz Delitzsch, the noted German theologian, suggests that the repeated admonition to comfort the people means it is both urgent and continuous. This idea of comfort after punishment and pardon, according to Delitzsch, forms the prologue for everything that follows in Isaiah. What follows is the announcement of how the comfort is to come.

<u>The Preparation for Comfort (vv. 3-5)</u>
Verses 3-5 were set to music by George Fredric Handel in his *Messiah* oratorio. He matched the sweeps of music to the heights of the mountains and depths of the valleys. The image has both a literal and figurative side. It was not unusual in Isaiah's day for the royal entourage literally to remake the landscape as it traveled. The king could not be troubled by climbing hills and descending into low places. Work would be done to make the way the king would travel as level as possible, even if it meant restructuring the countryside.

In his commentary Albert Barnes recounts the story of Semiramis, a queen of Babylon. As she was making her way into Media and Persia, she had to pass through a steep range of mountains with high peaks and narrow valleys in between. Rather than endure the hardships such a treacherous journey would bring, the queen ordered her caravan stopped while workers dug away the steepest parts of the hills and threw the dirt into the valleys until a straighter road was constructed for the queen, one that became "an everlasting memorial of herself."

The promise of such a highway through the desert must have been especially meaningful for the exiles in Babylon. Between them and their former homes lay miles of wilderness. But here was the voice of the prophet promising that their return would be treated as a triumphal march because God in all glory would be accompanying them as they moved toward Jerusalem, and everyone would see their victory. They would have nothing less than the very promise of God: "The mouth of the Lord has spoken" (40:5).

Figuratively, these words suggest the world-changing reality that God's coming brings. Part of the geography of Isaiah is the geography of the soul. If the glory of the Lord is to be revealed to all flesh, then the world must be prepared, changed, and reshaped so that everyone can see it together. Preparation for God's presence requires both inner and outer work, both individual and corporate work. The exiles in Babylon would have heard Isaiah's words both as promise and command.

The Need for Comfort (vv. 6-8)

The triumphal, cataclysmic work of highway building is interrupted, however, by the rest of the proclamation. Images of mountains crumbling into valleys, pictures of the revealed glory of God, give way to a metaphor of human life. The dialogue in verses 6-8 reminds readers that although the work of preparation is triumphant and victorious, the true dilemma of the human exile is mortality, the brevity of life, and the reality of death. If the mountains and valleys are to be moved, then what shall happen to human flesh, which is grass? It may wither and perish, but the promise of God endures forever.

This seems to be a reminder to those who have been in exile a long time. The promise has been given, but its fulfillment may be a long way off, so long, in fact, that some will fade like flowers and be gone before God's word will come to pass. The reality of death for human beings is set in sharp contrast to the eternal nature of God's promises. The prophet seems to be saying, "I know some of you are suffering and grieving. I know circumstances look as if the promises will never be fulfilled. But don't be discouraged. Love is on the way." In fact, it is because of the reality of death that the comfort and promises of God are so necessary.

The Appearance of Comfort (vv. 9-11)

If the promises of God are sure, then they can be prepared for without fear. We will not work in vain. We will not proclaim in vain. God will come. What has been promised will take place; now we can work to bring about the fulfillment. Lift up your voices, says the prophet. Don't fear. Proclaim loudly and clearly that God is here.

The image of God the prophet points to is twofold: the ruler and the shepherd. Both pictures must have spoken to the heart of the exiles in Babylon. Behold God, the powerful ruler who will defeat enemies, who will rule justly, who will reward generously, who will work diligently. After years of feeling abandoned, scattered, and powerless, God is coming as a ruler who will draw the people together, restore a sense of identity, and stay with them to work with them. The exiles taken as slaves into Babylon, isolated from their homes and place of worship, and deprived of freedom, will be led out by this victorious leader.

But God is not only pictured as a rescuing general. Behold God, the good shepherd. In a verse that echoes David's 23rd psalm and anticipates Jesus' own parable, Isaiah gives the weary exiles a picture of a God who is personal, compassionate, merciful, and nurturing. God cares for the young and the weak. God carries the helpless and hungry. God will gently lead.

Isaiah delivers a powerful and wonderful prophecy, secured by God's own promise. Preparations should be made, not just the same old routines, but earth-shaking changes must take place. Preparations should be made, not out of fear of disappointment, but in joy of anticipation and fulfillment. Love is on the way.

Sharing Our Connections

The message that came to the exiles comes down to each of us. The story of Christmas is so familiar to us that we often lose the sense of anticipation and wonder that accompanies it. For centuries the prophets had foretold the coming of the Messiah, and then it happened, when the fullness of time had arrived. Isaiah tells the exiles that comfort is coming, but the way must be prepared. This is both promise and command.

The weeks preceding Christmas are often ones of preparation. We must attend rehearsals, bake cookies, clean the house, hang the decorations, and, of course, wrap the presents. All of these preparations center around our families, churches, and communities. How often have we become so busy in preparing for these activities that we have not prepared ourselves spiritually?

In Isaiah's pictures the preparation that must be done is not a small task. Mountains must be leveled and valleys filled in. Everything crooked must be straightened; everything rough must be made smooth.

In the fourth-century church Advent was a period of fasting and confession, not unlike the forty-day period of Lent that precedes the celebration of Good Friday and Easter. It was a period to smooth what was rough and to straighten what was crooked in the soul. It was a period for reflection on what needed to be changed if the Christ was to be born anew within the heart that Christmas. In the spiritual geography of our souls, what earth-shaking changes need to take place? Advent is a good time to take inventory, to make preparations.

Advent is also a good time for reminding ourselves of the promises of God that are yet to be fulfilled. The birth of Jesus sets into motion the prophecies that will climax in the marriage feast in heaven pictured in the book of Revelation, when God will dry every tear, when all grief will be past, when there will be no sorrow or sickness or death. There will be no withering or fading away. It sounds like just another good story, just another pretty picture. But Isaiah's words come ringing down to us: "Lift up your voice with strength. Lift it up, do not fear; say . . . 'Here is your God.' " What promises of God are you waiting to have fulfilled? Advent is a good time to take inventory and to make preparations.

Expressing Our Faith

The image from stanza1 of our Advent hymn sees Love coming near us as a guest. "Make your house fair as you are able," says the hymnwriter. "Trim the hearth and set the table."

We understand about guests at Christmas time. Many of our homes will be opened for friends and family who will live with us overnight or for a few days. Cleaning the house, preparing the beds, and fixing the meals are all part of preparing a house for a guest. Often we as Christians picture ourselves as God's guest, eating at God's table in communion, visiting at God's house on Sunday. Advent asks us to consider how we would prepare ourselves if God were going to be our guest. The God who is coming to us is not coming in force. Instead, God is coming to us in love, as a guest. Our souls are God's room, our lives the scene of God's triumphal arrival.

It is so easy to move through the routine preparations of this season without making the kind of preparations Isaiah seemed to anticipate. Unlike children, for whom the approach of Christmas seems ever new and always special, we adults often find ourselves overshadowed with cynicism and despair over materialism, but we also find ourselves unable to change, to break out of the old ways of celebrating in order to find fresh new avenues of approach to this holy period.

Isaiah imagines breaking up the old paths, restructuring the roads we use to approach God and the ways we let God approach us. Inviting a guest into our homes is on some level like inviting the new into our old habits; it is inviting the potential for surprise into our daily routine. Allowing the anticipation for the coming of Christ to come into our lives may have the same effect. Old habits may get disrupted. Surprises may catch us offguard. And, just as we often discover with our own guests at Christmastime, we may find old friendship with God renewed and made richer. We may find our relationship with God taking on a new and glorious life.

The Second Sunday of Advent
Love the Rose Is on the Way

Isaiah 35:1-10

Core Highlights
• Christian Life
• Theology and Doctrine

Central Questions
• What role does surprise play in our understanding of God?
• What seeds have you planted in anticipation of God's blessings?

Focusing Our Vision
At the heart of the Advent stories is the element of surprise. Certainly the prophets had foretold the reality of a coming redeemer. But the promises had grown old as generation after generation had waited for fulfillment. Did many people still believe in the promises? Of course. But were they expecting fulfillment in their lifetime? Probably not.

We can only imagine the scene when the angel Gabriel appeared to announce to Mary her chosen status as the "handmaiden of the Lord." Perhaps like hundreds of other young Jewish women, she was busy with her housework. Perhaps she was cleaning or baking or weaving. As Luke recounts the story, the angel simply came into the room with the amazing message. As Charles H. Talbert pointed out in his commentary on Luke, the angel's announcement followed the established pattern, set both in Hebrew scriptures and in secular accounts, for the birth of a great person. On one hand, then, perhaps Mary would have recognized this divine pattern, but even if she did, there is no mistaking Luke's comment that she "was troubled," certainly a case of first-century literary understatement.

If we imagine ourselves at the scene, perhaps we come closer to the human emotion hidden under Luke's description. Not only would we be troubled; most of us would be stunned into disbelief. Some echo of that disbelief may echo in Mary's understandable question: "How can this be?"

In our Scripture text Isaiah builds a set of images around a promise no less amazing and unbelievable for the Jewish exiles. It comes immediately after what Robert Pinsky calls the "little apocalypse." Chapters 24–27 detail the awesome destructive power that God will unleash against Jerusalem and the rest of the world because of their unbelief. But throughout the apocalyptic language there is the underlying, quiet motif of a remnant that will survive and return to restore Jerusalem to its proper place. Pinsky, writing about this double-edged theme of destruction and restoration, commented: "Only the conviction of poetry can suspend these two ideas: God's just retribution and God's impenetrable 'strangeness,' in a single action." This "strangeness" of God is a quality that has been lost for many worshipers. It is, however, a strangeness that Mary and the other participants in the Advent narratives feel quite keenly.

The language Isaiah uses to talk about this promised return from exile in chapter 35 is the language of agriculture. These pictures would have been understandable pictures for Isaiah's audience even if many of us today are removed from the actual work of farming. But in this set of agricultural images we can see a forerunner of the image in stanza 2 of "People, Look East." "Love the Rose is on the way."

The appearance of a rose, even a rose like the wildflower known as the Rose of Sharon, is an unexpected surprise in the middle of the barren, arid wilderness. But, promises the prophet, there is coming a day when not only will there be a highway, but the desolate wilderness will burst into blossom. It will "blossom as the rose."

The Christmas Rose, common in the design of many stained-glass windows, is a reminder that Christ comes unexpectedly, surprisingly to us during this season, not unlike the unexpected surprising appearance of flowers in the dead of winter. The blooming of the rose is a tangible symbol of the fulfillment of God's promise. In medieval art depicting the annunciation, Mary is often pictured holding a lily to suggest her virginal purity. She might just as appropriately be painted holding a rose, the symbol of the Christ to come.

Listening to the Story

As Robert Pinsky reminds us, the language of Isaiah 35:1-10 is the language of poetry. The chapter anticipates the glorious day when the exiles from Babylon will once again make their way across the dessert to return to Jerusalem. But where the promise of a highway through the wilderness of Isaiah 40 can be seen literally, the blossoming desert that rejoices at the appearance of God's chosen is far more figurative.

The Glorious Consolation (vv. 1-2)

Joy is the overwhelming emotion of the opening voices. The wilderness and desert in prophetic writings were images both of desolation and testing, but also of spiritual revelation. John the Baptist lived in the wilderness as part of his ministry. Jesus was led into the wilderness to be tested. The arid wilderness areas of the Middle East were well known as places of danger and dryness. One had to prepare carefully to cross such an abandoned, inhospitable place. There was little here to welcome the traveler or to relieve the pilgrim.

Isaiah here proclaims, however, that with the return of the exiles these solitary, lonely places will rejoice and blossom. He personifies the land itself, suggesting that it will be so overcome, it will burst forth, not just into blossoms but also into songs. The idea that the created physical world responds to the presence of God's promises may seem entirely poetic in our scientific age, but Jesus used a similar image when confronted by priests on his entry into Jerusalem. When told to rebuke his disciples for their excessive celebrations, he replied, "I tell you that, if those should hold their peace, the stones would immediately cry out" (Luke 19:40). The rejoicing of creation, then, is directly connected to the earth recognizing its maker.

This joy will spread across the wilderness from Lebanon to Carmel and Sharon. In his commentary on Isaiah, Albert Barnes suggests that these three locations carry symbolic weight for the prophet.

> Carmel was emblematic of beauty, as Lebanon was of majesty, and as Sharon was of fertility . . . the sense is clear. The blessings of the times of the Messiah would be as great, compared with what had existed before, as if the desert were made as lovely as Carmel, and as fertile as Sharon.

This promise of restored power and beauty is a direct consolation to the devastation the prophet revealed in 33:9 where Lebanon, Carmel, and Sharon are left bare.

And it shall blossom "like the rose." The rose Isaiah foresees here is not, of course, our American roses noted for their multipetaled blossoms and sweet aromas. Instead, here is the rose of Sharon, a common wild-flower related to St. John's Wort and our modern hollyhocks. Its yellow and white petals and center of red would be quite noticeable in a desolate landscape, as would its evergreen leaves. Isaiah, then, imagines not a carefully cultivated rose garden in the desert, but rather a carpet of wild-flowers spreading across the arid plain, a symbol of the "glory of the Lord" that will be revealed.

The Necessary Response (vv. 3-4)

Just as we saw with our discussion of Isaiah 40 in the last lesson, the promise comes with responsibilities. The message to the exiles is one of active waiting. They are exhorted in verses 3-4 to act based on the picture of the deliverance promised in verses 1-2. Their actions are to take two basic forms. They are to strengthen and to speak.

Isaiah sees both of these actions as community-building actions. Those who hear the prophet's words are to work with those who are physically and spiritually weak, those who are about to give up hope, those who find the exile too hard to bear. The phrases "weak hands" and "feeble knees" may suggest the very young and the very old in the community, or they may refer symbolically to those whose actions and foundations are crumbling around them. The command to strengthen these carries with it the idea of encouragement, to give courage to them.

The message of encouragement is spelled out in the following verse. What can be said to those who are weak and failing? "Say to those . . . Be strong, do not fear. Here is your God." The message that God is coming is the message of Advent. Be strong; don't be afraid; love is on the way. Just as the blossoming rose reminds us that beauty and truth remain in the world, so it can remind us that God is coming to set the world right, to restore what was lost, to "save" us out of our exile.

The Amazing Results (vv. 5-10)

Isaiah's vision in chapter 35 climaxes with an amazing catalog of events that will result from the appearance of God. New Testament believers can find here many echoes of Jesus' earthly ministry, but there is also a sense in which we hear echoes of John's Revelation. Some of the promises here have yet to be fulfilled and will not be fulfilled until the end of the age. We can see from a list of the promises that what Isaiah sees is nothing less than a restoration of everything broken.

- The blind will see.
- The deaf will hear.
- The lame will leap.
- The wilderness will be watered.
- The holy highway will appear.
- The ransomed will return.

The first half of this list seems to refer to real physical ailments, those pressing difficulties that alter the quality of life for many and raise questions about God's care and provision. Here the prophet assures his listeners that when God comes, all will be made right with us. Our physical bodies with all their limitations and imperfections will be remade. Luke again records that Jesus reads a similar passage from Isaiah at the start of his public ministry and tells his astonished listeners that "today this scripture has been fulfilled in your hearing" (4:17-21).

The promise of individual healing, however, is only half of Isaiah's message. The other half is of corporate redemption. The holy highway of the Lord will appear. Here the highway seems not to be the literal, physical highway across the wilderness, but a symbolic highway where only the "wayfarers" who are "clean" and "not fools" will travel. On that road they will be preserved from the roaming lion of sin and those who would like to devour them. Instead of fear and failure, their travels will be marked by rejoicing and singing, just as the land itself has broken into blossom and song around them. On the other side of tragedy is joy. In the fulfillment of the promise is release from "sorrow and sighing."

Sharing our Connections

The church has often heard the words of Isaiah as referring not just to the return of the exiles from Babylon, but also in terms of the coming of Jesus the Messiah. In the thirteenth century the image of the rose of Sharon was used in Christian iconography as an image for Christ. This image was based primarily on the passage we have just studied from Isaiah and on a passage from the Song of Solomon.

This rich language and symbolism suggest to us that God can take root even in the barren ground where we find ourselves. Advent is the time of preparation. There is much to do and little time in which to do it. But psychologists tell us this is also a time of great depression and emotional paralysis for many people.

Some people are weakened by grief and disease. Some are hindered by emotional distress and broken relationships. Some are simply numb to the celebration being prepared around them. Some just go through the motions to prepare for another meaningless holiday. Some are acquainted intimately with the idea of the arid, desolate, isolated wilderness. These are the modern exiles, separated by choice or accident from the center of their spiritual strength. They may be afraid, close to giving up and giving in. They may be our friends or family; they may even be you and I.

Here are the words of promise in Isaiah's passage: The desert will blossom. The wilderness will sing. It does not seem possible now, but the most surprising things can happen when God finally appears. The promises may seem old and dusty until we realize that they might come true for us, now, in this season.

Like Mary, we could be going about our work and suddenly be in the presence of heaven. And if that happens, are we prepared, as Mary apparently was, to let God work? Or will our fear and cynicism and surprise paralyze us to what could be our blossoming hour? Can we prepare the ground for God's rose, even if the promised spring seems distant and the ground we have to turn over is frozen? Isaiah suggests there is a beautiful oasis just ahead, music just around the next corner. The joy is lying in wait for us to surprise our souls. Do we believe it?

Expressing Our Faith

In her essay "God in the Doorway" Annie Dillard, an American naturalist and essayist, recounts the story of her childhood fear of Santa Claus. She was afraid of Santa Claus, she says, because he seemed "to know when you were sleeping and to know when you're awake." Such power and intensity scared her so much that when a neighbor appeared at the family's doorway one Christmas dressed in the red suit and beard, young

Dillard ran screaming upstairs and refused to come down even for her presents. Then her essay takes an unexpected turn. That story, she suggests, is not unlike what happened at Christmas. "God came," she concludes, "and stood in the doorway, and we were all afraid."

Few of us as adults really welcome surprises. We are too aware that surprises can be negative as well as positive. Often surprises are things we did not and could not plan for that cause us to rethink and reorder our lives. Many of us would prefer to continue in our ordinary way of doing things, perhaps not even noticing a messenger of God if one should appear in our doorway. A flower that blooms out of season is better ignored than wondered at because it might be a sign of God's approaching presence. An emotional response to a Christmas carol or story is best wiped away before someone notices and accuses us of being childlike.

But Isaiah invites us into the wonder that the appearance of God always brings with it. Suddenly we open our eyes to see the desert being transformed into a garden. Suddenly a way opens before us where there had only been struggle before. Suddenly there is music where there had only been weeping. Those who have experienced such transforming miracles are encouraged to strengthen those of us who are still fearful and feeble. We need to hear the promises again that God will remove the sorrow and sighing from our lives and that God will come to be with us to restore us and, yes, even to save us. We need to be reminded during this season of preparation that love is indeed coming to us, like a guest, like a rose. We need to prepare our hearts.

The Third Sunday of Advent
Love the Bird Is on the Way

Deuteronomy 32:7-12

Core Highlights
• Christian Life
• Theology and Doctrine

Central Questions
• What keeps us from being gathered under God's wings?
• How has your life grown toward responsible independence in God?

Focusing Our Vision
The most familiar bird image to most Christians is the appearance of the Holy Spirit "like a dove" in the accounts of Jesus' baptism. But that reference to a bird builds upon several images of birds that would have been familiar to the witnesses of Jesus' baptism. Birds were part of the sacrificial system. Noah had released birds at the end of the deluge to search for dry land. Even God had been compared to a bird, as in our session text for today.

Birds have always held a special fascination for human beings. These flying creatures have been symbols of freedom, peace, and even in one memorable Alfred Hitchcock movie, of fear. But for many of us, our associations with birds are far simpler. We enjoy their music. We may teach some to mimic our words. We may even keep them as pets. But the birds that truly inspire us are those in the wild, the ones we observe in nature.

As a child I remember peering intently into a bush growing beside my parents' house. There, hidden in the branches, was a tiny twig nest, lined with wispy feathers. On the bed of down lay three pale, sky blue eggs. It was a robin's nest.

Robins were important to us in northern Pennsylvania. Their appearance heralded the end of winter and the return of warmer weather. Their songs predicted rain showers. And their constant searching told aspiring fishermen where the worms were.

The robins kept their nests all that long spring as my brother and I watched. Finally, the eggs opened. In their place were crying hungry baby birds. Then the feeding began. The robins caught the food, chewed it for the helpless young, and fed it to them until they grew strong. Suddenly, one day, without our expecting it, the nest was empty. The parents and children were gone. Just as quietly as they had come, they left, having raised their children to the time of flight.

We often use the language of birds to describe the cycles of our lives. We talk about "taking flight" and "nesting." We even talk about "empty nest syndrome" to describe the empty feeling parents experience when their children leave home. The language of birds is also biblical language.

Listening to the Story

Moses has come to the end of his long ministry of leading and exhorting the children of Israel. At the end of the book of Deuteronomy (literally the "second law," referring to the repetition of the commandments also found in Exodus), Moses delivers his closing discourse in which he rehearses the history of the children of Israel up to his own day and reminds them of how God has behaved toward them. Then he delivers his final exhortation as they stand poised to enter the Promised Land. The narrative refers to this as "Moses' song" (31:30). It is his final song, a poem actually, one that attempts to present the people with memorable and informative word pictures.

One of the word pictures Moses develops is of God as a bird, an eagle, rescuing the people from the wilderness. In building this metaphor Moses is actually building on God's own language from Exodus 19:4. "You have seen what I did to the Egyptians, and how I bore you on eagles' wings and brought you to myself." Moses seizes upon this divinely revealed metaphor for his own remembrances of the flight from slavery in Egypt.

Remembering the Situation (vv. 7-9)

Moses' intention in his discourse is to aid the memory of the people. Throughout the Hebrew Scriptures the people are encouraged to actively remember, to rehearse the history, as a way of strengthening their faith and choosing the right paths for the future. Moses commands the children of Israel to "remember," not as a way of avoiding present action or future challenges, but as a way of guiding that action and meeting those challenges. The story Moses is recounting is to be preserved and repeated.

One of the benefits many churches find in observing the seasons of the Christian year is exactly that element of repeating and preserving the story. Beginning with Advent and the anticipation of the coming of Christ, and on through Christmas, Epiphany, Lent, Holy Week, Easter, and Pentecost, every year the church hears again the story of God's redemption of God's people. Far from being an exact repetition, of course, each time the story deepens the experience and exposes new elements.

For the children of Israel on the shores of the Jordan about to cross over into the land that has been promised to them, the experience of remembering is a necessary discipline. Moses' words are clear. It is God who has ordained the course and boundaries of the nations. It is God who is in control of the international relationships, but remember, you are God's people. You are not a free and independent state able to make your own alliances; you are God's portion. Remember to whom you belong. Remember your family connections. Remember, Moses says, that you are the Lord's portion—God's share.

The act of remembering in that way becomes a spiritual discipline that helps the people to act in accordance with God's will. This same theme is echoed in John's revelation to the church at Ephesus:

> But I have this against you, that you have abandoned the love you had at first. Remember then from what you have fallen; repent, and do the works you did at first. (Rev 2:4-5)

This spiritual remembering forms the basis of our own individual life narratives. We remember what life was like, where we were, what we were doing, and how we were behaving before we came into God's family. Such remembering is good for us.

Some birds operate with a kind of memory. Their migratory patterns are passed from generation to generation. Birds rest in the same ponds and forests, nest in the same areas, and travel the same paths year after year. A disruption in the natural landscape can lead to confusion and danger for the entire flock. Remember, Moses tells the people, whose flock you are.

Picturing the Story (vv. 10-12)

Moses then builds on the image of the mothering eagle God revealed in Exodus 19:4. He seems to be answering two questions: What should be remembered? Why should it be remembered?

What should be remembered is both the original condition of the people and the reality of God's deliverance. Once again the image of the wilderness serves as a setting for the condition of the people. Here the people are exiles from Egypt, nomads journeying across the desert in hopes of some future land, some future permanence that will be a nation, a homeland.

Moses' language here to describe the wilderness is extreme: it is a barren, howling waste. The Hebrew word "waste" is the same word found in Genesis 1:2 and translated there as "without form." The people were lost in a formless, barren existence—no purpose, no means of direction, no hope of survival. They were in a desert with no landmarks, no roads, and no food. Symbolically, the picture is of more than the literal experience of being lost in a desert. Moses seems to be pointing to the spiritual reality of a people who was not yet a people. They were merely a group of desert nomads, milling about with no higher direction or purpose.

The other item that should be remembered, according to Moses, is the action of God's deliverance. These people wandering in the wilderness are "found." In their commentary on this passage, Keil and Delitzsch expand this word picture:

> Finding presupposes seeking, and in the seeking the love which goes in search of a loved one is manifested . . . It was in that [desert] situation that the Lord surrounded His people . . . To surround them with love and care, not merely to protect them . . . to pay attention, in the sense of not to lose sight of them. "To keep as the apple of the eye" is a figurative description of the tenderest care.

To be found when we are hiding or lost is one of the great joys of life. Being found implies that we are worth looking for, that we are part of a whole that will be lessened by our absence. Being found means that we are valued and missed. Moses asks the people to remember that when they were aimless wanderers, lost in the wilderness, then they were found by God, guided and guarded, protected and loved. What a wonderful memory to hold and rehearse!

To underscore the narrative, Moses turns to the image of God as the great eagle. God as the mother eagle tends the nest, protecting and nurturing the young birds, watching and "hovering" over them. Then the day of flight training arrives. The mother eagle bears the young ones up on her wings, carrying them on her back, until they spread their own wings and take flight. Then the Lord becomes a leader, directing the now independent fledglings toward the goal.

In one short verse Moses is able to develop a metaphoric picture of God's dealings with the people. There is a sequential narrative moving from the helplessness of birth to the independence of flight. There is growth and development in the relationship between God and the people. It is like the growth cycle of birds, who are initially protected and fed within the confines of the nest, but are eventually encouraged to find their wings and take flight to follow the parents on their journey.

Moses closes his word picture with a reminder that the Lord alone has done this. No other god would stoop to helpless weakness. No other god would protect and feed. No other god would teach and guide. "The Lord *alone* guided." It is for that reason the story should be remembered. It reveals a remarkable picture of God as a caring, nurturing, guiding parent. It is the same maternal image that Jesus revises on the Mount of Olives as he approaches his own death: "Jerusalem, Jerusalem, the city that kills the prophets and stones those who are sent to it! How often have I desired to gather your children together as a hen gathers her brood under her wings, and you were not willing" (Matt 23:37).

Sharing Our Connections
Throughout the winter on their farm in northern Pennsylvania, my parents keep a bird feeder filled with sunflower seeds. In the mornings and in the evenings the winter birds, often only chickadees and the loud bluejays, flock to feed. Every now and then there will be flash of scarlet. A cardinal will appear amid the ruckus. It is a moment that always raises a

shout within the house. "Come see the redbird!" It is a flash of color and beauty in the winter landscape. Like roses, the appearance of birds in the dead of winter, during December, during Advent time, is unexpected.

Moses' image of God as an eagle means that God's people are the fledgling birds. In the metaphorical story we find ourselves in two different positions. We are early the helpless newborns, completely dependent upon the nurturing, protective power of the parent. Later, however, we are expected to find our own wings and to fly with the parent, following God, as it were, on our flight.

The image might remind us of the ancient myth of Dadealus and Icarus, as recounted in Ovid's *Metamorphoses*. Dadaelus, the skilled craftsman, has been imprisoned by the king of Crete. In order to escape, he fashions wings for himself and for his son, Icarus. After sewing the wings to the body of his son, Dadealus instructs him in the art of flight and exhorts him to fly the middle path between the sun and the earth. The rest of the story is all too familiar. Icarus, overcome with the intoxicating joy and freedom of flight, sores upward toward the sun, only to realize too late that the heat has melted the feathers from the wingframes. Calling his father's name, he tumbles into the ocean. Dadealus, as Ovid describes the tale, frantically searches for his son until he looks down and sees the feathers, floating in the water.

Being a bird, the story suggests, brings both freedom and responsibility. Just as God chooses to be responsible toward the fledgling nation, so they must be responsible in their flight. They are to follow where God alone leads them. Like the children of Israel, our own freedom of flight, spiritually, should be disciplined by our remembering of our own story of how God has found us and taught us to fly. We need to allow ourselves to be gathered under God's wings. We need to focus our attention on God alone.

Expressing Our Faith

Stanza 3 of "People, Look East" imagines that the empty nest of the spring birds will suddenly be filled with new life. Here in "the hour when wings are frozen/God for fledging time has chosen."

We have been discussing in these lessons the preparation that must take place during the season of Advent. Just as the bird must prepare the nest, collecting twigs, weaving them together, lining the nest with its own feathers in anticipation of the coming of the young birds, so we must prepare for the coming of Christ who will nest within each of us. The return of the robins each April herald the return of spring and new life. Here in the cold season of winter we are encouraged to remember, to rehearse, the story of God's coming into the cold and barren wilderness of this world. The coming of God as a child, a baby who needed to be protected and nurtured, reminds us of our own human condition. Like baby birds, we grow from complete dependence to responsible independence under God. In the Christian life we find the vital tension that keeps our faith alive: how to remain dependent upon God, willing to be gathered under the wings, and how to fly independently in our own faith, choosing to follow our guide.

Advent, then, is a time to prepare our "nests" for the celebration of Christmas, not just the houses in which we live, but also our inner sanctuaries where Christ makes a home. But it is also a time to remember our own stories of being found in the wilderness of life, of being nurtured and fed, and of learning to fly strong so that we can in turn nurture others. As Moses reminded the people, that story is not just a good story to remember; it is a story that must be remembered. We need always to remind ourselves "whose we are."

The Fourth Sunday of Advent
Love the Star Is On the Way

Revelation 1:9-20

Core Highlights
• Christian Life and Worship
• Theology and Doctrine

Central Questions
• How are we continuing to prepare for Christ's coming into this world?
• How are we guiding others toward a knowledge of Christ?

Focusing Our Vision
Waiting for the arrival of a loved one is often a difficult task. I remember as a child waiting for my father to come home from work or waiting for my mother to return from her errands. Time seemed to crawl by. Each minute until the time of expected arrival seemed to last at least an hour. I knew they were coming, but I wanted to see them so much that it seemed as if they would never come. What if they had forgotten? What if they didn't return?

John, the beloved disciple, might have had similar feelings during his exile on the island of Patmos, a prison island off the coast of Asia Minor that the Romans used to house people who were deemed dangerous to the community. John's presence on the island suggests he was in trouble for preaching the gospel. Instead of being killed by the authorities, he had been transported to the island to live out his days. He lived, however, in expectation of the coming of Christ. "The time [of fulfillment] is near," he reminds his readers (1:3).

"The time of fulfillment" is a phrase also used in connection with the Advent narratives. Paul reminds the Galatian church that "when the fullness of time had come, God sent his son" (Gal 4:4). Luke uses similar language in the birth narrative: "While they were there, the time came for her to deliver her child" (2:6). John, writing several decades after the Christmas event, repeats the same language. This time, however, it refers to the second coming, the return of Jesus to redeem the world.

133

Advent, by its nature as the season wherein we anticipate Christ's coming, has always had a dual focus in the church. It is the season of preparation for the Christmas feast to be sure, but it also has eschatological overtones because we as 21st-century Christians find ourselves in a similar position with many of the 1st-century believers. The prophecies of Christ's coming are promises to be sure, but where is his coming?

In our text the risen Christ comes to John on the island of Patmos in a surprising and unmistakable way. This is John's call to prophesy a message for the churches, a message that has been preserved through the centuries. With it comes a picture, an image, of Christ who burns away all of our preconceptions.

Listening to the Story
Exactly why John is on the island of Patmos is not clear. There is no indication in the text of severe persecution he has suffered or any acts of physical violence. He does speak of enduring suffering, but he may be in exile as a kind of Roman protection, simply removing him from those who would do him harm. He does connect his imprisonment to his preaching and his testimony. For whatever reason, he has become an exile. Like the children of Israel in Egypt, and like the Judean exiles in Babylon, John is looking for redemption, a chance to return, to reconnect with the family of faith. As with those former groups, the message is clear: Love is coming to you. Love will find you and lead you home. Love comes for John in the vision of the resurrected Christ.

The Call (vv. 9-12)
John the exile takes pains to connect his own experience to the experiences of the churches who are his audience. I have shared with you, he says, the "persecution and the kingdom and the patient endurance" of being in Christ. He calls himself their brother. The language of family connections within the church has become so widespread today that the metaphorical impact of such language is often lost. John claims family connections here. He is their sibling, an equal to them, and they are equal to him. What happens to one member of a close family happens to them all. That includes exile and exhilaration.

In his exile, on the Lord's Day (a term that refers to Sunday, a way the early Christians used to distinguish their day of worship from the traditional Sabbath), John is "in the spirit." This phrase carries with it the sense of prophetic trance and also serves to isolate John, just as the earlier language had served to connect him. To our ears, the phrase "in the spirit" has strange, mystical overtones. Other translations render this phrase "the spirit came over me," which carries with it the idea of possession and does little to help us understand it. Perhaps we are best left with the idea that John, while conducting his ordinary weekly worship, suddenly has an encounter with the divine that breaks through the ordinary. Like Mary going about her housework, John suddenly finds himself in the very presence of God.

The voice thunders and trumpets. This is a voice not to be ignored. It breaks through the silence of ritual and repetition. It demands attention. It is a call to action, and the action is to "write." Unlike other prophets throughout the Scriptures who were commanded to "go" and to "speak," John is commanded to "write." There on his island home, his world circumscribed by the pounding surf, John's prophetic call is a particularly literary one. His communication of what he sees will be through the written word.

John's audience for this writing is to be the now famous "seven churches" of Asia Minor. Much has been written about why these seven churches are particularly mentioned here. Even the casual reader will recognize the names of "Ephesus" and "Laodicea" as appearing in other New Testament contexts. As with all prophetic messages, the specific audiences are both literal and symbolic. The letters to the churches that follow in chapters 2 and 3 of this book are site specific. They address specific situations occurring in each of these congregations. It is interesting to note that the list given in verse 11 arranges the churches in the geographical order in which they appeared on the northern route that led from Ephesus to Laodicea. John is picturing in his mind the physical highway that stretches through the region and imagining the route his epistle will physically take.

He must also know, however, that the epistle will encounter other churches and other believers along the way. This list of seven, while specific and literal, also is meant to symbolize the church in that entire region. In his commentary on the Revelation, G. R. Beasley-Murray suggests that the churches represent "the church of Christ in the whole world." This universality is also underscored by the appearance of the seven lampstands. This image hearkens back to a passage from the prophet Zechariah. Zechariah had a vision of a single lampstand with seven bowls, each of which represented those who were faithful to God (4:2ff). John sees each of the seven churches as a separate lamp, suggesting that each church represents the faithful before God. Each church becomes a microcosm of the universal church.

The One Who Calls (vv. 13-20)

Ultimately the lamps are not the focus of John's vision, however. For there, walking among the lamps is an amazing, burning, bright figure. The picture of the risen Christ owes much to the portraits of God found in the Hebrew scriptures, particularly Daniel's vision of the Ancient of Days in chapter 7. Several dominant characteristics emerge in John's descriptions.

First, Christ appears as a priest. The long robe and gold girdle call to mind the costume of the high priest. The priest is the intercessor for the people, the one who comforts and mediates for the congregation. The long robe reaches to the feet instead of being tucked up into the girdle. Being untucked suggests that Christ has completed his labor and is now serving regally in the heavenly temple.

Second, Christ appears in light. The repetition of "white" and "white as snow," or of "fire" and "burnished bronze," suggests an image almost difficult to look at in its brightness. The risen Christ is shining, almost burning with light. This light, of course, suggests power and purity. It also suggests the piercing nature of illumination and revelation. Simeon in the temple prophesied that the infant Christ would be a "light to the Gentiles" (Luke 2:32). Here is that prophecy made almost painfully real.

Third, the images associated with Christ are images of power. His voice is a thundering voice, "the sound of many waters." A sword flashes in his mouth, and he carries seven stars, again symbolic of the seven churches, in his hand. The voice perhaps suggests the beginning of creation where through the spoken word Christ in God created light and all the known universe. The sword suggests the discerning, cutting power of

Christ's words on earth, the "sword of the Spirit" Paul alludes to in Ephesians 6:17. And he is carrying the seven churches, representing all the churches. He is sustaining them, guarding them. They are stars in a single constellation, bound together by their nature and by their place in Christ's hand. Christ is shining as a star, and the churches reflect that powerful, burning starlight.

Christ's words shift John's vision away from the present circumstances and onto the eternal, powerful person who is guiding the present situation. "I am the first and the last, and the living one. I was dead, and see, I am alive forever and ever; and I have the keys of Death and of Hades" (vv. 17-18). Here is the powerful revelation of Christ's self-identity. He speaks of eternity past and future. He speaks of the incarnation, death, and resurrection. He speaks of the future judgment. Here is the image of the one who has been from the beginning and will be forevermore. Here is the one who heard the cries of the Israelites in Egypt and led them out in the Exodus. Here is the one who comforted the Babylonian exiles and promised them a highway through the desert. The road, however, is one not around suffering and exile and death, but through suffering and exile and death. As Beasley-Murray notes:

> The new exodus which the redeemer came to achieve entailed both death and resurrection, and by this twin event he brought about an emancipation which included liberation from guild and participation in the eternal kingdom.

It is on the basis of Christ's identity that the second command to "write" is given to John. "Write what you have seen, what is, and what is to take place after this" (v. 19). This command encompasses everything that follows in the book, and again underscores the eternal quality of the risen Christ. Christ knows what is and what will be. He is guiding the future events that will climax later in the book with a triumphal coming to earth again. This is the message to the churches. Love is coming, coming in priestly power and victory, coming like a burning blazing star.

Sharing Our Connections
Such a mystical, literal prophetic vision seems removed from most of our experiences. While such images and pictures of God are inspiring, they

are also a bit overwhelming since they are beyond most of our experiences. In some sense the same is true of the Advent narratives. Mary's visitation by the angel, Joseph's directive dreams, the shepherd's midnight angel chorus, the Magi's heavenly sign—all of these speak to a world where the supernatural and the natural are much more closely intertwined than our own. Few, if any, of us expect a prophetic vision as we sit in morning worship or pray in our private devotionals. That is simply not our world.

Lying on my back, on the grass of my parent's lawn in Pennsylvania, looking up at the night sky, the stars seem a brilliant but distant beauty. I can trace the familiar constellations, Orion, the Big and Little Dippers, and Cassiopeia. I know from many science classes and much reading that each of those distant points of light represents a blazing, fusion furnace of incredible power and energy. Yet, in the darkness at the end of a hard day's work, they seem just little distant pinpricks, beautiful but harmless.

Sometimes the image of Christ revealed in John's writing seems as distant and harmless as those stars. I know that God is powerful and creative and will one day bring this age to an end. But the prophecies and promise seem far away and distant. Like the stars in the night sky, space and time minimize their reality. Advent is a season of the Christian year that plunges us back into the reality, the possibility of Christ's coming. If we believe that Christ once came into this world as a human infant, then we might also believe that Christ could return. And if we believe that Christ could return, then God becomes much more immediate to us. Christ is the first and last, and by implication, Christ is at every moment in between—even our own moment, even right now, even this minute.

If we get too close to Christ, however, we might find ourselves burning away, just as we would if we approached a physically burning star. In our text John falls down as though he were dead. To believe in such a Christ is to find ourselves overcome by such a vision. Or, if we might extend John's picture one step further, we might find ourselves ignited as stars. Like the seven churches who burn initially as lamps at Christ's feet and finally as stars in God's hand, we might find ourselves ablaze with the life of the risen Christ.

An old Jewish legend recounts the story of a disciple who approached the old rabbi, Abba Joseph. "I have kept all of the commandments," said the disciple. "I have kept the fasts and the feasts. I have done all of my prayers. I have cleansed my body and my mind. I have lived righteously. Now what shall I do?" The old rabbi stood up before the disciple and stretched his hands up toward heaven. Flames appeared at the ends of each finger leaping up toward God. "Why don't you be totally changed into fire?" he replied.

Expressing Our Faith

Christmas is almost here, and with the Christmas story comes the emphasis on the Christmas star, that strange heavenly event that guided the Magi on their journey from the east to Bethlehem. That heavenly event, commonly referred to as a "star," was somehow representative of the Christ child himself. The magi knew that a divine king had been born.

For centuries stars have been used as guides for navigation and travel. Boy Scouts and Girl Scouts today often learn to tell directions on night camping trips based on the stars, particularly by finding the brilliant North Star. Recently a car company even named its onboard guidance system "the Northstar system."

John's vision of the risen Christ burning like the daystar of the morning reminds us of the direction in which we as Christians are spiritually traveling. The way out of the exile of this world is marked for us by the risen Christ who shines before us as guide and guard. The way through the wilderness can be tracked by marking that star.

But John's vision also makes clear that the churches themselves, and by extension, the members of those churches, are to become like stars. Connected to the risen Christ, held and guarded in his hand, the churches are to burn like guiding stars in constellations, revealing the power and plan of God. Too often, however, churches burn dimly and distantly, like those faraway physical stars in the night sky. They reveal no pattern, no plan; they would not direct any seeking person to the newborn king.

Can you see yourself as a star? Can you see your church as part of the constellation that directs others toward the risen, returning Christ? Can you anticipate during this Advent season the appearance and rebirth of Christ in your own heart and soul? Have you, like Abba Joseph's disciple, lived the righteous life and observed all of the law? Are you ready, then, to be turned into fire?

Intergenerational

The First Sunday of Advent
Love the Guest Is on the Way

Welcoming the stranger may be opening our lives to people in our church who are not known because of differences in age, gender, or lack of opportunity. The following exercise provides an opportunity for brief but possibly significant opportunities for meeting new people.

Divide the entire group into two groups. Ask the members of one group to form an inside circle, turning their backs to the center. Instruct the other group to form a circle around the inside circle, facing the center. Have each person line up with another person, making a double circle. Give the following instructions.

> *For a period of time we will share feelings and experiences about being guests, hosts, friends, and strangers. Every two minutes I will announce a topic for discussion. Each time I announce a new subject, if you are in the inside circle, move to the left one person. In this way each of you will share some of your experiences with many different people in the entire group.*

Possible Topics
- Describe a time when you have had guests in your home.
- Describe a time when you have been a guest in another home.
- How does your home change during the Christmas season?
- How does your church change during the Christmas season?
- What are your favorite Christmas decorations?
- What have you been taught about meeting strangers?
- In what sense is Jesus a stranger?
- In what sense is Jesus a close friend?
- How do you respond to people you do not know very well?
- Do you remember strangers being in your home at Christmastime?
- What are some ways you prepare for the birth of Christ?
- What are some ways your family prepares for the birth of Christ?

The Second Sunday of Advent
Love the Rose Is on the Way

Prepare a smell and memory activity using a variety of strongly scented items. Seal each item in a separate bag. Number and label each bag.

Suggested Items
• lemons
• onions
• pineapple
• coffee grounds
• peppermint candy
• dried flowers or potpourri
• cinnamon sticks
• whole cloves
• cotton balls soaked with scented oils (vanilla, peach, pine)
• a fresh rose

Describe ways the sense of smell is used in the Bible. Divide the group into dyads (pairs). Distribute paper and pencil to one person in each dyad. Blindfold the other person. Introduce each blindfolded person to each distinct smell. Ask him/her to identify the smell. Ask the other person in the dyad to record responses for each item. When all have finished recording their responses, display the contents of the bags. Give group members correct responses. Call for persons to share specific memories evoked from the different scents.

Focus attention on the rose. Pass it around for each person to smell. Call for reactions and memories evoked. Discuss ways that this specific fragrance enhances our lives and worship. Thank God for the gifts of smell and memory.

The Third Sunday of Advent
Love the Bird Is on the Way

Imagine that Jesus has gathered us together "like a mother bird has gathered her chicks." What kind of gathering is this? Imagine the room as a "nest" where all are gathered in one place. The task is to behold the intergenerational group in all its sizes, shapes, ages, and combinations.

Use a large room with plenty of open space. Ask the group to stand in a circle, pretending it is a clock. At your direction have persons move to a certain "time" segment on "the clock." For instance, have the shortest (or oldest) people in the group stand between 12:00 and 1:00. Others will follow around the circle, positioning themselves according to height (or age). The tallest (or oldest) will be standing between 11:00 and 12:00. Other circle formations could be based on birthdays or alphabetical groupings of first or last names. After each circle formation, allow adequate time for persons to "behold" or "see" the group this way. In closing, ask the following questions:

- What do you see when the church family is gathered in these different formations?
- As a result of these formations, do you now see people in a different light?
- Have you met some people you didn't know before?

The Fourth Sunday of Advent
Love the Star Is on the Way

Find a place where there are many sensory images, preferably the outdoors at night or the early dawn, with live animals nearby. Read the following guided meditation slowly, giving long pauses between phrases. After the meditation, ask persons to form groups of three or four and share their responses.

Let us begin this time together in silence. Close your eyes. Relax your body by taking deep breaths. As you exhale, imagine letting go of all the hurried, busy thoughts and feelings. Sit comfortably with your body relaxed and your mind alert.

Now open your eyes slightly so you can see vague objects through your eyelashes. Imagine you are seeing all this for the first time. You do not have names for what you are seeing—only observations about size, shape, and color.

Very slowly open your eyes wide. Take in a full view of your surroundings. Behold everything around you. Again, observe without naming or describing. Continue to remind yourself that you are seeing all of this for the first time. Begin to think about what your eyes are continually drawn toward, what the environment holds that seems to have the most interest and fascination. Follow your eyes more than your thoughts.

Now fix your eyes on the one object or person that holds your attention. Study that object or person carefully with your eyes. Ask yourself these questions: How did that object or person come to be, and why in this particular location? How long has this object or person been here? What would this object or person tell us about this place?

In your imagination continue to communicate with what or who you are seeing in any way that seems to be effective. Now spend a few moments thinking about all you have experienced and how you would describe all of this to others.

Bibliography

Books

Adam, David. *The Cry of the Deer: Meditations on the Hymn of St. Patrick.* London: SPCK, 1987.

Banks, Robert. *God the Worker.* Valley Forge PA: Judson Press, 1994.

Barnes, Albert. *Notes on the Old Testament: Isaiah,* 53-56, 502. Grand Rapids: Baker Book House, 1983.

Beasley-Murray, George R. *John,* 11. Vol. 36, *Word Biblical Commentary.* Waco: Word Books, 1987.

_____. *New Century Bible Commentary: The Book of Revelation,* 66-68. Grand Rapids: Wm. B. Eerdman Publishing Co., 1974.

Berry, Wendell. "The Wild Rose." In *Entries.* Pantheon Books, 1994. Originally published in *Kentucky Poetry Review* (New York: Pantheon Books, a division of Random House).

Buechner, Frederick. *The Magnificent Defeat.* New York: HarperCollins, 1966.

Buettner, Gudrun, ed. *The Audubon Society Encyclopedia of Animal Life,* 89. New York: Clarkson N. Potter, Inc., 1982.

Delitzsch, Franz. *Biblical Commentary of the Prophecies of Isaiah.* Translated by James Martin. Grand Rapids: Wm. B. Eerdmans Publishing Co., 1954.

Dillard, Annie. "God in the Doorway." In *Teaching a Stone to Talk: Expeditions and Encounters.* New York: Harper & Row Publishers, 1982.

Farjeon, Eleanor. "People, Look East." In *Oxford Book of Carols.* Oxford: Oxford University Press, 1964. Published in *Hymns, Psalms, and Spiritual Songs.* Louisville KY: Westminster/John Knox Press, 1990.

Finkelstein, Louis. "Nothing Is Ordinary." In *The Ways of Religion: An Introduction to the Major Traditions,* 270-71. New York: Oxford University Press, 1993.

Hopkins, Gerard Manley. *Poems.* Edited by W. H. Gardner and N. H. Mackenzie, 69. New York, Oxford University Press, 1967.

Johnson, Joan. "A Prayer for Each Day's Journey." In *Laughter, Silence, and Shouting. An Anthology of Women's Prayers,* edited by Kathy Keay, 36-37. London: HarperCollins Publishers, 1994.

Keil, C. F. and F. Delitzsch. *Biblical Commentary on the Old Testament: The Pentateuch,* 471-72. Translated by James Martin. Grand Rapids: Wm. B. Eerdmans Publishing Co., 1956.

McBroom, Amanda. *The Rose.* Secaucus NJ: Warner-Tamerlance, 1977.

Pinskey, Robert. "Isaiah." In *Congregations: Contemporary Writers Read the Jewish Bible,* edited by David Rosenberg, 144-60. New York: Harcourt, Brace, Jovanovich, 1987.

Shea, John. *An Experience Named Spirit,* 257-60. Chicago: Thomas More Press, 1983.

Simpson, Evelyn M., and George R. Potte, eds. *The Sermons of John Donne.* Berkley and Los Angeles: University of California Press, 1962.

Stewart, Sonja M., and Jerome W. Berryman. *Young Children and Worship.* Louisville KY: Westminister/John Knox Press, 1989.

Stookey, Laurence Hull. *Calendar: Christ's Time for the Church*, 23-24. Nashville: Abingdon Press, 1996.

Talbert, Charles H. *Reading Luke: A Literary and Theological Commentary on the Third Gospel*, 18. New York: Crossroad, 1989.

Choral Works

"Lo, How a Rose E'er Blooming." Arranged by Dennis Allen. In *The Music of Christmas*, 42-47. Genevox, 1996.

"Prepare Ye the Way of the Lord." Words and music by Dennis and Nan Allen. In *The Music of Christmas*, 35-40. Genevox, 1996.

Instrumental Works

"A Christmas Medley." Arranged by Salvatore A. Buouo. In *Pedalpoint* (October-December 1988): 19. Nashville: Broadman Press, SESAC.

"Good Christian Men, Rejoice." Arranged by Barry Brama. In *I Know That My Redeemer Lives*, 22. Nashville: Broadman Press 1980.

"Hark! the Herald Angels Sing." Arranged by Martha Kelsey. In *Pedalpoint* (October-December 1996): 28. Nashville: Broadman Press, SESAC.

"In the Bleak Midwinter." Arranged by Marilynn Ham. In *I Would Do My Part: A Christmas Medley*, 30. Kansas City: Lillenas Publishing Co., 1988.

"Infant Holy, Infant Lowly." Arranged by Terry Honeycutt. In *Pedalpoint* (October-December 1991): 22. Nashville: Broadman Press, 1991.

"It Came Upon a Midnight Clear," Arranged by Stan Pethel. In *Pedalpoint* (October-December 1994): 24. Nashville: Van Ness Press, Inc., ASCAP.

"O Come, O Come, Emmanuel." Arranged by John H. Campbell. In *Amazing Grace*, 7. Nashville: Broadman Press, 1985, SESAC.

"Of the Father's Love Begotten." Arranged by Wilbur Held. In *The Organist's Manual*, 145. New York: W. W. Norton and Co., 1985.

"Once in Royal David's City." Arranged by Mike Sharp. In *Pedalpoint* (October-December 1984): 22. Nashville: Broadman Press, SESAC.

"Sing We Now of Christmas." Arranged by Samuel Wellman. In *Pedalpoint* (October-December 1993): 10. Nashville: McKinney Music, Inc., BMI.

"Sonata of Christmas." Arranged by Don Wyrtzen. In *Sonatas of Praise*, 48. Nashville: Van Ness Press, Inc., 1994.

"Still, Still, Still." Setting by Paul Manz. In *Improvisations for the Christmas Season*, Set 2, 12. St. Louis MO: MorningStar Music Publishers, 1987.

"The First Nowell." Arranged by Stan Pethel. In *All That Thrills My Soul*, 18. Nashville: Broadman Press, 1983.

"To Shepherds as They Watched by Night." Setting by Paul Manz. In *Ten Chorale Improvisations*, Set 2, 16. St. Louis: Concordia Publishing House, 1964.

Other available titles from

#Connect
Reaching Youth Across the Digital Divide
Brian Foreman

Reaching our youth across the digital divide is a struggle for parents, ministers, and other adults who work with Generation Z—today's teenagers. *#Connect* leads readers into the technological landscape, encourages conversations with teenagers, and reminds us all to be the presence of Christ in every facet of our lives. *978-1-57312-693-9 120 pages/pb* **$13.00**

1 Corinthians (Smyth & Helwys Annual Bible Study series)
Growing through Diversity
Don & Anita Flowers

Don and Anita Flowers present this comprehensive study of 1 Corinthians, filled with scholarly insight and dealing with such varied topics as marriage and sexuality, spiritual gifts and love, and diversity and unity. The authors examine Paul's relationship with the church in Corinth as well as the culture of that city to give context to topics that can seem far removed from Christian life today. *Teaching Guide 978-1-57312-701-1 122 pages/pb* **$14.00**
Study Guide 978-1-57312-705-9 52 pages/pb **$6.00**

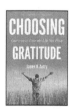

Choosing Gratitude
Learning to Love the Life You Have
James A. Autry

Autry reminds us that gratitude is a choice, a spiritual—not social—process. He suggests that if we cultivate gratitude as a way of being, we may not change the world and its ills, but we can change our response to the world. If we fill our lives with moments of gratitude, we will indeed love the life we have. *978-1-57312-614-4 144 pages/pb* **$15.00**

Choosing Gratitude 365 Days a Year
Your Daily Guide to Grateful Living
James A. Autry and Sally J. Pederson

Filled with quotes, poems, and the inspired voices of both Pederson and Autry, in a society consumed by fears of not having "enough"—money, possessions, security, and so on—this book suggests that if we cultivate gratitude as a way of being, we may not change the world and its ills, but we can change our response to the world. *978-1-57312-689-2 210 pages/pb* **$18.00**

Contextualizing the Gospel
A Homiletic Commentary on 1 Corinthians
Brian L. Harbour

Harbour examines every part of Paul's letter, providing a rich resource for those who want to struggle with the difficult texts as well as the simple texts, who want to know how God's word—all of it—intersects with their lives today.   *978-1-57312-589-5 240 pages/pb* **$19.00**

Dance Lessons
Moving to the Beat of God's Heart
Jeanie Miley

Miley shares her joys and struggles a she learns to "dance" with the Spirit of the Living God.   *978-1-57312-622-9 240 pages/pb* **$19.00**

A Divine Duet
Ministry and Motherhood
Alicia Davis Porterfield, ed.

Each essay in this inspiring collection is as different as the mother-minister who wrote it, from theologians to chaplains, inner-city ministers to rural-poverty ministers, youth pastors to preachers, mothers who have adopted, birthed, and done both.

978-1-57312-676-2 146 pages/pb **$16.00**

The Enoch Factor
The Sacred Art of Knowing God
Steve McSwain

The Enoch Factor is a persuasive argument for a more enlightened religious dialogue in America, one that affirms the goals of all religions—guiding followers in self-awareness, finding serenity and happiness, and discovering what the author describes as "the sacred art of knowing God."   *978-1-57312-556-7 256 pages/pb* **$21.00**

Ethics as if Jesus Mattered
Essays in Honor of Glen H. Stassen
Rick Axtell, Michelle Tooley, Michael L. Westmoreland-White, eds.

Ethics as if Jesus Mattered will introduce Stassen's work to a new generation, advance dialogue and debate in Christian ethics, and inspire more faithful discipleship just as it honors one whom the contributors consider a mentor.   *978-1-57312-695-3 234 pages/pb* **$18.00**

To order call **1-800-747-3016** or visit **www.helwys.com**

Healing Our Hurts
Coping with Difficult Emotions
Daniel Bagby

In *Healing Our Hurts*, Daniel Bagby identifies and explains all the dynamics at play in these complex emotions. Offering practical biblical insights to these feelings, he interprets faith-based responses to separate overly religious piety from true, natural human emotion. This book helps us learn how to deal with life's difficult emotions in a redemptive and responsible way. 978-1-57312-613-7 *144 pages/pb* **$15.00**

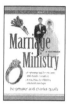

Marriage Ministry: A Guidebook
Bo Prosser and Charles Qualls

This book is equally helpful for ministers, for nearly/newlywed couples, and for thousands of couples across our land looking for fresh air in their marriages. 1-57312-432-X *160 pages/pb* **$16.00**

Hope for the Thinking Christian
Seeking a Path of Faith through Everyday Life
Stephen Reese

Readers who want to confront their faith more directly, to think it through and be open to God in an individual, authentic, spiritual encounter will find a resonant voice in Stephen Reese.

978-1-57312-553-6 *160 pages/pb* **$16.00**

A Hungry Soul Desperate to Taste God's Grace
Honest Prayers for Life
Charles Qualls

Part of how we *see* God is determined by how we *listen* to God. There is so much noise and movement in the world that competes with images of God. This noise would drown out God's beckoning voice and distract us. Charles Qualls's newest book offers readers prayers for that journey toward the meaning and mystery of God. 978-1-57312-648-9 *152 pages/pb* **$14.00**

I'm Trying to Lead... Is Anybody Following?
The Challenge of Congregational Leadership in the Postmodern World
Charles B. Bugg

Bugg provides us with a view of leadership that has theological integrity, honors the diversity of church members, and reinforces the brave hearts of church leaders who offer vision and take risks in the service of Christ and the church. 978-1-57312-731-8 *136 pages/pb* **$13.00**

To order call **1-800-747-3016** or visit **www.helwys.com**

James M. Dunn and Soul Freedom

Aaron Douglas Weaver

James Milton Dunn, over the last fifty years, has been the most aggressive Baptist proponent for religious liberty in the United States. Soul freedom—voluntary, uncoerced faith and an unfettered individual conscience before God—is the basis of his understanding of church-state separation and the historic Baptist basis of religious liberty. *978-1-57312-590-1 224 pages/pb* **$18.00**

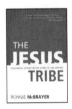

The Jesus Tribe

Following Christ in the Land of the Empire

Ronnie McBrayer

The Jesus Tribe fleshes out the implications, possibilities, contradictions, and complexities of what it means to live within the Jesus Tribe and in the shadow of the American Empire.

978-1-57312-592-5 208 pages/pb **$17.00**

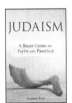

Judaism

A Brief Guide to Faith and Practice

Sharon Pace

Sharon Pace's newest book is a sensitive and comprehensive introduction to Judaism. What is it like to be born into the Jewish community? How does belief in the One God and a universal morality shape the way in which Jews see the world? How does one find meaning in life and the courage to endure suffering? How does one mark joy and forge community ties? *978-1-57312-644-1 144 pages/pb* **$16.00**

Let Me More of Their Beauty See

Reading Familiar Verses in Context

Diane G. Chen

Let Me More of Their Beauty See offers eight examples of how attention to the historical and literary settings can safeguard against taking a text out of context, bring out its transforming power in greater dimension, and help us apply Scripture appropriately in our daily lives.

978-1-57312-564-2 160 pages/pb **$17.00**

Living Call

An Old Church and a Young Minister Find Life Together

Tony Lankford

This light look at church and ministry highlights the dire need for fidelity to the vocation of church leadership. It also illustrates Lankford's conviction that the historic, local congregation has a beautiful, vibrant, and hopeful future. *978-1-57312-702-8 112 pages/pb* **$12.00**

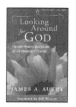

Looking Around for God
The Strangely Reverent Observations of an Unconventional Christian
James A. Autry

Looking Around for God, Autry's tenth book, is in many ways his most personal. In it he considers his unique life of faith and belief in God. Autry is a former Fortune 500 executive, author, poet, and consultant whose work has had a significant influence on leadership thinking.

978-157312-484-3 144 pages/pb **$16.00**

Making the Timeless Word Timely
A Primer for Preachers
Michael B. Brown

Michael Brown writes, "There is a simple formula for sermon preparation that creates messages that apply and engage whether your parish is rural or urban, young or old, rich or poor, five thousand members or fifty." The other part of the task, of course, involves being creative and insightful enough to know how to take the general formula for sermon preparation and make it particular in its impact on a specific congregation. Brown guides the reader through the formula and the skills to employ it with excellence and integrity.

978-1-57312-578-9 160 pages/pb **$16.00**

Meeting Jesus Today
For the Cautious, the Curious, and the Committed
Jeanie Miley

Meeting Jesus Today, ideal for both individual study and small groups, is intended to be used as a workbook. It is designed to move readers from studying the Scriptures and ideas within the chapters to recording their journey with the Living Christ.

978-1-57312-677-9 320 pages/pb **$19.00**

The Ministry Life
101 Tips for New Ministers
John Killinger

Sharing years of wisdom from more than fifty years in ministry and teaching, *The Ministry Life: 101 Tips for New Ministers* by John Killinger is filled with practical advice and wisdom for a minister's day-to-day tasks as well as advice on intellectual and spiritual habits to keep ministers of any age healthy and fulfilled.

978-1-57312-662-5 244 pages/pb **$19.00**

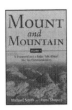

Mount and Mountain
Vol. 1: A Reverend and a Rabbi Talk About the Ten Commandments
Rami Shapiro and Michael Smith

Mount and Mountain represents the first half of an interfaith dialogue—a dialogue that neither preaches nor placates but challenges its participants to work both singly and together in the task of reinterpreting sacred texts. Mike and Rami discuss the nature of divinity, the power of faith, the beauty of myth and story, the necessity of doubt, the achievements, failings, and future of religion, and, above all, the struggle to live ethically and in harmony with the way of God.   *978-1-57312-612-0 144 pages/pb* **$15.00**

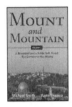

Mount and Mountain
Vol. 2: A Reverend and a Rabbi Talk About the Sermon on the Mount
Rami Shapiro and Michael Smith

This book, focused on the Sermon on the Mount, represents the second half of Mike and Rami's dialogue. In it, Mike and Rami explore the text of Jesus' sermon cooperatively, contributing perspectives drawn from their lives and religious traditions and seeking moments of illumination.   *978-1-57312-654-0 254 pages/pb* **$19.00**

Of Mice and Ministers
Musings and Conversations About Life, Death, Grace, and Everything
Bert Montgomery

With stories about pains, joys, and everyday life, *Of Mice and Ministers* finds Jesus in some unlikely places and challenges us to do the same. From tattooed women ministers to saying the "N"-word to the brotherly kiss, Bert Montgomery takes seriously the lesson from Psalm 139—where can one go that God is not already there?   *978-1-57312-733-2 154 pages/pb* **$14.00**

Overcoming Adolescence
Growing Beyond Childhood into Maturity
Marion D. Aldridge

In *Overcoming Adolescence*, Marion D. Aldridge poses questions for adults of all ages to consider. His challenge to readers is one he has personally worked to confront: to grow up *all the way*—mentally, physically, academically, socially, emotionally, and spiritually. The key involves not only knowing how to work through the process but also how to recognize what may be contributing to our perpetual adolescence.

978-1-57312-577-2 156 pages/pb **$17.00**

Quiet Faith
An Introvert's Guide to Spiritual Survival
Judson Edwards

In eight finely crafted chapters, Edwards looks at key issues like evangelism, interpreting the Bible, dealing with doubt, and surviving the church from the perspective of a confirmed, but sometimes reluctant, introvert. In the process, he offers some provocative insights that introverts will find helpful and reassuring. *978-1-57312-681-6 144 pages/pb* **$15.00**

Reading Ezekiel (Reading the Old Testament series)
A Literary and Theological Commentary
Marvin A. Sweeney

The book of Ezekiel points to the return of YHWH to the holy temple at the center of a reconstituted Israel and creation at large. As such, the book of Ezekiel portrays the purging of Jerusalem, the Temple, and the people, to reconstitute them as part of a new creation at the conclusion of the book. With Jerusalem, the Temple, and the people so purged, YHWH stands once again in the holy center of the created world.

978-1-57312-658-8 264 pages/pb **$22.00**

Reading Hosea–Micah
(Reading the Old Testament series)
A Literary and Theological Commentary
Terence E. Fretheim

Terence E. Fretheim explores themes of indictment, judgment, and salvation in Hosea–Micah. The indictment against the people of God especially involves issues of idolatry, as well as abuse of the poor and needy. The effects of such behaviors are often horrendous in their severity. While God is often the subject of such judgments, the consequences, like fruit, grow out of the deed itself. *978-1-57312-687-8 224 pages/pb* **$22.00**

Sessions with Genesis (Session Bible Studies series)
The Story Begins
Tony W. Cartledge

Immersing us in the book of Genesis, Tony W. Cartledge examines both its major stories and the smaller cycles of hope and failure, of promise and judgment. Genesis introduces these themes of divine faithfulness and human failure in unmistakable terms, tracing Israel's beginning to the creation of the world and professing a belief that Israel's particular history had universal significance. *978-1-57312-636-6 144 pages/pb* **$14.00**

Sessions with Revelation (Session Bible Studies series)
The Final Days of Evil
David Sapp

David Sapp's careful guide through Revelation demonstrates that it is a letter of hope for believers; it is less about the last days of history than it is about the last days of evil. Without eliminating its mystery, Sapp unlocks Revelation's central truths so that its relevance becomes clear. 978-1-57312-706-6 *166 pages/pb* **$14.00**

Silver Linings
My Life Before and After *Challenger 7*
June Scobee Rodgers

We know the public story of *Challenger 7*'s tragic destruction. That day, June's life took a new direction that ultimately led to the creation of the Challenger Center and to new life and new love. Her story of Christian faith and triumph over adversity will inspire readers of every age. 978-1-57312-570-3 *352 pages/hc* **$28.00**
978-1-57312-694-6 *352 pages/pb* **$18.00**

Spacious
Exploring Faith and Place
Holly Sprink

Exploring where we are and why that matters to God is an ongoing process. If we are present and attentive, God creatively and continuously widens our view of the world. 978-1-57312-649-6 *156 pages/pb* **$16.00**

The Teaching Church
Congregation as Mentor
Christopher M. Hamlin / Sarah Jackson Shelton

Collected in *The Teaching Church: Congregation as Mentor* are the stories of the pastors who shared how congregations have shaped, nurtured, and, sometimes, broken their resolve to be faithful servants of God. 978-1-57312-682-3 *112 pages/pb* **$13.00**

Time for Supper
Invitations to Christ's Table
Brett Younger

Some scholars suggest that every meal in literature is a communion scene. Could every meal in the Bible be a communion text? Could every passage be an invitation to God's grace? At the Lord's Table we experience sorrow, hope, friendship, and forgiveness. These meditations on the Lord's Supper help us listen to the myriad of ways God invites us to gratefully, reverently, and joyfully share the cup of Christ. 978-1-57312-720-2 *246 pages/pb* **$18.00**

To order call **1-800-747-3016** or visit **www.helwys.com**

A Time to Laugh
Humor in the Bible

Mark E. Biddle

An extension of his well-loved seminary course on humor in the Bible, *A Time to Laugh* draws on Mark E. Biddle's command of Hebrew language and cultural subtleties to explore the ways humor was intentionally incorporated into Scripture. With characteristic liveliness, Biddle guides the reader through the stories of six biblical characters who did rather unexpected things. 978-1-57312-683-0 *164 pages/pb* **$14.00**

The World Is Waiting for You
Celebrating the 50th Ordination Anniversary of Addie Davis

Pamela R. Durso & LeAnn Gunter Johns, eds.

Hope for the church and the world is alive and well in the words of these gifted women. Keen insight, delightful observations, profound courage, and a gift for communicating the good news are woven throughout these sermons. The Spirit so evident in Addie's calling clearly continues in her legacy. 978-1-57312-732-5 *224 pages/pb* **$18.00**

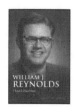

William J. Reynolds
Church Musician

David W. Music

William J. Reynolds is renowned among Baptist musicians, music ministers, song leaders, and hymnody students. In eminently readable style, David W. Music's comprehensive biography describes Reynolds's family and educational background, his career as a minister of music, denominational leader, and seminary professor. 978-1-57312-690-8 *358 pages/pb* **$23.00**

With Us in the Wilderness
Finding God's Story in Our Lives

Laura A. Barclay

What stories compose your spiritual biography? In *With Us in the Wilderness*, Laura Barclay shares her own stories of the intersection of the divine and the everyday, guiding readers toward identifying and embracing God's presence in their own narratives.

978-1-57312-721-9 *120 pages/pb* **$13.00**

54461612R00096

Made in the USA
Lexington, KY
17 August 2016